SECOND PART

v

FOREWORD

In our society, everyone is looking for ways to improve their physical fitness. Yet, while people do plenty of exercises to train their bodies, they hardly do anything to train their minds.

But it is absolutely crucial to practice a mental fitness program, if you want to keep your brain in good shape!

Get Your Brain in the Fast Lane has been conceived as a complete training program for the brain, with more than 130 exercises that call upon your skills in five main cognitive areas:
- memory
- language
- attention and concentration
- logical reasoning
- visual and spatial acuity

Even if you feel more comfortable using some cognitive skills more than others, challenge them all, as they are all very useful in daily life.

This book is not just entertainment for your brain; it is a workout to make your brain as efficient as it can be, honing the skills that you use in your daily life.

A certain degree of attention and focus are required for this program. So find a quiet place where you can concentrate before beginning *Get Your Brain in the Fast Lane*.

Finally, take a few minutes to read the introduction of the book for an explanation of how to count your points and evaluate your score.

iii

The authors

CONTENTS

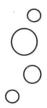

INTRODUCTION

How to use this book

Get Your Brain in the Fast Lane was conceived as a training program that progresses over levels of increasing difficulty. It is made up of two main parts or levels:
- Level#1 will enable you to warm up your neurons with relatively easy exercises.
- Level#2 comprises more difficult exercises that you should try after you have finished part one.

Get Your Brain in the Fast Lane is a comprehensive program that trains the five main cognitive areas. A colored shape on each page indicates what cognitive area is at work in each exercise:

- Memory ▨
- Language ▥
- Attention and concentration ▥
- Logical reasoning ▨
- Visual and spatial acuity ▥

In order for you to recognize your weaknesses and strengths, each exercise is scored. At the end of each part of the book, you can count your total points and get some useful comments on your results:
- A general comment about your general performance,
- A detailed comment about each cognitive area.

When you compare your results at the end of the easiest part and then at the end of the most difficult part you will realize how you have progressed since you started the training!

Before starting the exercise it is best to read the next few pages carefully. They will explain the main cognitive functions and provide some practical advice for training your brain in your daily life.

Happy Training!

SOME PRACTICAL ADVICE ─────────

To be able to read and understand an article in a magazine, write a note with a pen, recognize a friend in a crowded shop, remember the first and last name of your son's friend, make a mathematical calculation, have a conversation with your neighbor, button your shirt, know that a rose is a flower, remember where you have parked your car, know how to ride a bike . . .

. . . The list is endless! All these activities and knowledge require your brain to be in good shape. The basis of a fit brain are mental capacities also known as cognitive functions.

The main cognitive functions are: **attention, memory, language, logical reasoning, visual and spatial acuity.**

Even though we spend valuable time and money to maintain a healthy body—exercising, eating right, getting the proper amount of sleep—and even though studies have proved that mental stimulation improves cognitive functioning, we often neglect our most valuable organ: the brain.

What is good for your body is also good for your brain. For instance, a balanced diet is absolutely necessary for optimal brain functioning, as the brain requires glucose, vitamins, and unsaturated fatty acids. Regular exercise is necessary for blood flow that carries oxygen to the brain, and a good night's sleep enables you to learn new things and process daily tasks. Tobacco use, excessive alcohol consumption, and too much stress not only prevent our bodies from performing well, they also impair our brain functioning. When we take care of our bodies by eating well, getting enough sleep and exercise, and avoiding harmful behavior patterns, we also take care of our brains.

However, when it comes to the brain, the one factor we often neglect is mental stimulation. We are creatures of habit and tend to engage in the same activities and behavior patterns. These routine activities do not stimulate or benefit the brain.

In fact, the brain "prefers" novelty and unexpected events. As humans, our cognitive functions thrive and improve when we're faced with new ideas, events, and challenges. When we mentally challenge ourselves on a regular basis, we can maintain good intellectual potential as well as reduce our risk for age-related memory loss.

SOME PRACTICAL ADVICE ————

ATTENTION

Attention is necessary in nearly all daily tasks. It enables you to focus on the task at hand, learn and understand information, and concentrate on something.

Your capacity to concentrate is highly dependent on changes in the environment or in yourself (noise, stress, concern, tiredness, disruptive thoughts, etc.).

Good attention enables you to maintain concentration despite noise and distractions and to concentrate on several activities at once. For instance, you can simultaneously drive and have a discussion with your passenger. As we age, our attention span can decrease, making us more susceptible to distractions and less efficient at multi-tasking.

MEMORY

Memory is essential in your daily life. You constantly call upon it for various reasons—to remember a PIN, a phone number, the title of a movie, an appointment, where you put your keys, a historical event, etc. It also plays a crucial role in all cognitive activities, including reading, reasoning, and mental calculation.

We constantly rely on memory to learn, remember childhood and personal experiences, and use the motor skills necessary for daily life. Memory is deeply entwined with our personality, as it holds all of the experiences that make us who we are.

Because memory is integral to our lives, memory loss can be a painful experience. However, memory loss is in fact quite rare. While our cognitive performance may decrease as we age, it rarely affects our quality of life. Various factors can affect our memory in addition to age; extreme tiredness, stress, or lack of motivation can all be detrimental to memory.

To maintain a good memory, you need to train the multiple facets of your memory.

Short-term memory enables you to store seven items of information (plus or minus two) for about one minute. For instance, you can remember the list of items you have to buy for the time it takes you to write

SOME PRACTICAL ADVICE

down your grocery list. It is crucial when you read, enabling you to remember what you have just read and thereby understand the logical flow of sentences and the meaning of the text.

On the other hand, long-term memory enables you to store information for an unlimited amount of time. The quantity of information that may be stored in your long-term memory is also unlimited. Long-term memory can be stored in different forms:

An *episodic memory* stores your personal memories and the events that happened in your own life, like last Christmas party, your appointment with the bank, or last summer vacation.

Semantic memory stores general knowledge such as grammar rules, mathematical operations, word definitions, and the names of countries or objects. Unlike episodic memory, semantic memory is not linked to any particular memorization context. Semantic memory enables you to remember a fact without referencing the context in which you learned it.

Procedural memory allows you to store motor skills and learned tasks, such as driving, tying your shoe, or playing an instrument.

LANGUAGE

Every day you use the various aspects of oral (understanding and expression) or written (reading and writing) language. For instance, when you talk, you create sentences, using appropriate words from your vocabulary. You don't say these words in just any order but organize them according to the rules of grammar.

When you write a letter or a report, you also use grammar and spelling, and you try to find synonyms to avoid repeating the same word too often. When you read, you analyze the words and ascertain the key words that will help you grasp the meaning of the text and remember it.

Reading continuous text is a succession of steps, sentence after sentence, paragraph after paragraph. To understand such a text, you must keep in mind (temporarily) the information read in each sentence. This brings you to the next step: the next sentence or paragraph. Most people, however, cannot remember each sentence exactly as it appears in the text. Only the most relevant information is stored (and for a longer

SOME PRACTICAL ADVICE

time). This enables you, for example, to write a summary. At the same time, irrelevant, redundant, and contradictory information is erased from your memory to avoid overload and ultimately enable you to determine the general meaning of the text.

LOGICAL REASONING

Your logical reasoning capacities help you solve little or big problems every day. Without even realizing it, you use your reasoning skills on a daily basis to make decisions, build up hypotheses, and consider the possible consequences of your actions.

Your reasoning capacities enable you to react appropriately to unusual situations or to create strategies when faced with unexpected events, such as when your computer displays an error or your chess adversary makes a surprising move.

Naturally, when you have to solve a new problem you often try to use a solution that had worked to solve a similar problem. But you may not always be 100% successful!

The various steps necessary to carry out a reasoning task are:
- problem analysis
- setting up the goal
- developing a strategy and action plan to solve the issue.

Several steps are necessary for your brain to reason successfully. After analyzing a problem and defining your goal, you must determine a strategy and an action plan to solve the problem and reach your goal. If the goal is too difficult to reach in a single step, you must define intermediate objectives to make progress easier. At the same time, it is necessary to take into account the means available to you and to consider the constraints and processes that follow. Finally, it is crucial to select an appropriate solution when several solutions are available and to make sure that your action plan will indeed achieve your goal.

Therefore, good logical reasoning is primarily the application of good methodology!

MASTERING SPACE AND MENTAL IMAGERY

We live in a colorful, three-dimensional world. In order to recognize an object's position in relation to other objects (below, above, on the right, on the left) or estimate the distance between you and something you need to constantly analyze the shape and color of things. Analyzing visual information is necessary to be able to act within your environment.

Your visual system utilizes two distinct parts of your brain:
- the first one analyzes the shape of objects,
- the second one analyzes their spatial properties (size, location, orientation).

These two brain parts work together to transform all of the shapes and spatial properties into a unique visual landscape that you can understand.

Mental imagery is a cognitive activity that enables you to perceive something when this something is not actually present or happening. You "see" something in your mind. Visual analysis and mental imagery have numerous similarities, but only mental imagery allows you to transform an object—for instance, to rotate it—in your imagination.

Chess players frequently use mental imagery to evaluate the consequences of possible moves as they mentally simulate moving a piece without actually touching it. Mental imagery goes by other names too such as dreaming, reasoning, and mental calculation.

HOW CAN WE MAINTAIN OUR COGNITIVE FUNCTIONS

As we age, our ability to concentrate decreases, and we aren't able to execute standard mental operations as quickly as we did when we were younger. We may also have difficulty remembering recently acquired words.

Cognitive aging is usually attributed to the progressive loss of neurons (the cells that conduct nerve impulses), but neuron loss is less important than it was thought to be a few years ago. We're discovering that more important than the number of neurons is the intensity of their connections—intensity that can be strengthened through mental stimulation.

Recent scientific studies have shown that activities that require taking initiative and careful planning, like gardening and traveling, are associated with a decreased risk of developing Alzheimer's disease. Other studies have shown that it's better for the mind to engage in manual activities, such as do-it-yourself projects, painting, gardening,

SOME PRACTICAL ADVICE ——————

playing an instrument, and participating in sports, than it is to watch television, attend meetings, and listen passively to conversations.

To maintain sharp cognitive skills, it is necessary to vary your intellectual activities on a regular basis, and the exercises in *Get Your Brain in the Fast Lane* can help you do just that!

PRACTICAL ADVICE

Here are some practical tips and commonsense recommendations that will help you acquire good habits for maintaining your cognitive capacities on a daily basis—without a lot of effort!

Practice the art of focusing

In order to remember something, it is often useful to focus on what is being done as memorization occurs. For example, if you read a text without focusing, it is very likely that you will not remember a word of it. Similarly, if you have just put your glasses in an unusual place without consciously thinking "I am putting my glasses on the kitchen table near the vase," the chances are good that you will not immediately find them when you look for them.

Motivation can also play a critical role in focusing. For example, you may read a book about the geography of Spain. Your memorization of the information will be much greater if you read the book because you are going to visit the country or if your son is moving there. The same principle applies to practice. If you read information about how to ride a horse—but never ride one—you will likely forget most of what you've read. If you ride horses, however, practice will imprint the information of the book in your brain.

Mentally repeat the information you want to memorize

Studies have shown that repeating information that you have just learned helps to ensure its transfer into long-term memory, where it is more likely to be remembered. Memory is strengthened by repetition.

Think about the information you want to memorize

Asking yourself questions about the information you want to memorize increases the probability that it will eventually be stored in long-term

SOME PRACTICAL ADVICE ─────────

memory. It deepens your understanding of the information, which is the basis of memorization. For example, you have a better chance of remembering that eating fat is bad for the heart if you wonder "why is it bad for the heart?", and an even greater chance if someone gives you an explanation. A deeper understanding of information makes it logical and clear in your mind, as well as more likely to be committed to memory.

Sum up the information

Making a summary of the information you need to retain enables you to extract its essential elements without overloading your short-term memory with unimportant details.

Organize the information you want to learn

Classifying the information you want to learn is also a useful step in memorization, especially when you have to remember a large amount of information, like a long shopping list.

When you organize information into logical categories (for instance, vegetables and dairy products), the memorization process becomes easier. Instead of remembering individual words, you remember the names of categories, and what is in the categories themselves will be retrieved more easily. Instead of remembering seven or eight items, you remember two categories, in which there are three or four items each. For example, if you go shopping, rather than trying to remember to buy tomatoes, lettuce, toothpaste, cake mix, ice cream, soap, and beans, try to remember three vegetables, two desserts, and two bathroom items. Remembering the category will trigger retrieval of what is in that category.

To memorize a string of numbers—like a telephone or credit card number—it is helpful to divide the numbers into pairs or groups of four. You can then link them to birth dates or other significant historical events that are familiar to you and that you can easily retrieve.

Create acronyms

Mnemonic devices like acronyms help make the process of memorization easier. If you use them regularly, they become efficient tools. For example, in memorizing a list of words, you can make up an

SOME PRACTICAL ADVICE ——————————

acronym from their first letters, so that each letter acts as a trigger for the retrieval of the words.

Turn routine tasks into rituals

In order not to lose your keys, glasses, or important letters, you should always put an object in the same place, and—even better—in a place that is related to its function. In the same way, in order not to forget daily tasks, like watering plants or taking medications, you should perform them at the same time each day and use external time "landmarks" as an aid. For instance, if you always water the plants after the postman delivers the mail, you have an external cue to help you remember to do it!

Use spatial and temporal landmarks when retrieving information

Making note of spatial and temporal landmarks during the learning process is highly beneficial in helping you retrieve information later. For instance, if you want to remember where you have parked your car, it is very helpful to make a specific note of something distinctive in the surroundings, like a fire hydrant or a lamppost. To remember an itinerary along city streets that you aren't familiar with, turn around at regular intervals to visualize the return route. In this way, you can memorize visual elements in both directions—and lessen your chances of becoming lost when you return along the same route.

Create associations

Creating associations relating several items will help you memorize them. To learn a list of words, for instance, you can build a sentence or phrase that associates several words in the list. You can also associate a word with a familiar location or with an object in that location. To remember a PIN, for example, you can relate the number (or each digit thereof) to a birth date, the number of your street, your age, or other important number.

For optimal results, use these strategies while you work the exercises in this book. Soon, you'll find yourself applying them to everyday life!

FIRST PART

Exercises: level #1

The solutions are on page 175.

RIGHT OR WRONG?

In this exercise you will have to remember various items that you may have learned or read a long time ago (long-term memory) in varied fields such as history, art, sport, chemistry, etc.

Decide whether the following statements are right or wrong.

1 - Spiders are insects.

2 - *Moby Dick* was written by Herman Melville.

3 - Christmas is on December 26th.

4 - Tees are accessories to play golf.

5 - Christopher Columbus was Italian.

6 - The chemical symbol for silver is: Ag.

7 - Thailand is a European country.

8 - Mark Knopfler is a member of the Rolling Stones.

9 - Tiger Woods is a golf player.

10 - The flag of Great Britain has five colors.

11 - Marilyn Monroe acted in *Some Like It Hot*.

12 - The approximate value of pi is 3.1416.

13 - Some inhabitants of Germany are called Hamburgers.

14 - Virginia Woolf was American.

15 - Fur is made of animal skins.

16 - Montreal is the capital of Canada.

17 - J. F. Kennedy was born in 1920.

18 - Britney Spears wrote "Like a Virgin."

19 - Brazil and Bolivia have a common border.

20 - Cathedrals are Catholic churches.

You need at least fifteen right answers to get one point. ■

RIGHT OR WRONG?

Decide whether the following statements are right or wrong.

1 - *Romeo and Juliet* was written by Shakespeare.

2 - Katrina was a hurricane.

3 - The Koran is the holy book for Jews.

4 - Roses can be black.

5 - Squares have four sides.

6 - Leukemia is a skin disease.

7 - Margaret Thatcher was a Prime Minister of Ireland.

8 - Alaska is a state of the USA.

9 - Highlands are mountains of Switzerland.

10 - The moon is a planet.

11 - Audrey Hepburn received an Oscar posthumously.

12 - La Paz is the capital of Peru.

13 - Sushi is a Japanese food.

14 - Squirrels are mammals.

15 - The Battle of Wounded Knee happened in 1900.

16 - "Gonna" is the abbreviation for "going to."

17 - Cherries grow on trees.

18 - The humerus is a bone of the leg.

19 - Unicorns are horses with wings.

20 - Aristotle was an actor.

4

You need at least fifteen right answers to get one point.

SINGULAR OR PLURAL?

This exercise will sharpen your vocabulary and require you to classify words according to two different criteria: singular or plural and alphabetical order.

This grid contains eight singular and eight plural nouns. Can you sort them out?

women	glasses	children	cheese
feet	geese	foxes	stairs
tribe	criterion	nail	box
sketches	hemisphere	shoe	sock

In this grid, classify the words as singular or plural and write them down in alphabetical order.

Singular	Plural

5

If you have not made more than one error, you get one point. ■

SINGULAR OR PLURAL?

This grid contains eight singular and eight plural nouns. Can you sort them out?

halves	crane	speed	silver
eyelash	people	mice	bear
teeth	city	excess	mouse
supplies	thieves	prices	sins

In this grid, classify the words as singular or plural and write them down in alphabetical order.

Singular	Plural

If you have not made more than one error, you get one point. ▥

TOWERS OF HANOI

This is a problem-solving exercise. **To perform this exercise, you must determine the best strategy by calculating the fewest number of moves to reach your objective.**

Determine the fewest number of moves necessary to change the configuration in Figure A to that shown in Figure B. You must observe these rules:

- You may not place a larger disk on a smaller one.
- You may move only one disk at a time.

A

B

If you have found the fewest number of moves necessary, you get one point. ■

TOWERS OF HANOI

Determine the fewest number of moves necessary to change the configuration in Figure A to that shown in Figure B. You must observe these rules:

- You may not place a larger disk on a smaller one.
- You may move only one disk at a time.

A

B

If you have found the fewest number of moves necessary, you get one point. ■

CHIVALRY

This exercise trains your:
- Visual memory
- Visual exploration capacities
- Visual concentration

Take a careful look at the shape, the colors, and the patterns of the shield below. Then turn the page to continue.

9

CHIVALRY (continued)

Select the various elements that make up the shield on the preceding page.

Choose its shape:

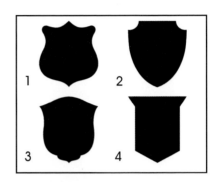

Choose its colors:

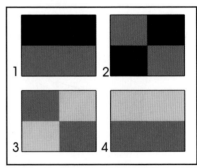

Choose its pattern:

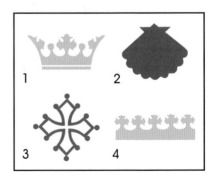

If the shield is identical, you get one point. ■

CHIVALRY

Take a careful look at the shape, the colors, and the patterns of the shield below. Then turn the page to continue.

CHIVALRY (continued)

Select the various elements that make up the shield on the preceding page.

Choose its shape:

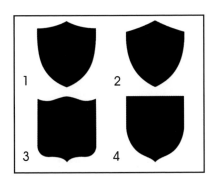

Choose its colors:

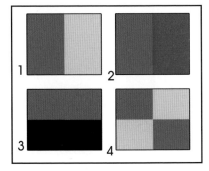

Choose its pattern:

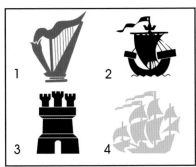

If the shield is identical, you get one point.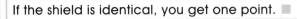

THE LAST WORD

This set of exercises will train your working memory while you engage in reading. Working memory helps you to temporarily keep certain items in mind while you are processing them. It involves processing what is read and heard, and it enables you to store words and meanings for a short period of time.

> Carefully read the following four sentences and try to memorize the last word of each sentence. Then turn the page to continue.

1 - The class was delayed because the teacher ran out of gas.

2 - After one week, his brother had still not fixed the computer.

3 - Peter and Sara went to Greece on their honeymoon.

4 - Lisa wore the green sweater she had been given for her birthday.

THE LAST WORD (continued)

Now try to answer the following questions.

What was the color of Lisa's sweater?
- blue
- green
- black

Write down the last word of each sentence:

Sentence #1: _____

Sentence #2: _____

Sentence #3: _____

Sentence #4: _____

Please check your answers against the previous page.

If you have not made any errors, you get one point.

THE LAST WORD

> Carefully read the following four sentences and try to memorize the last word of each sentence. Then turn the page to continue.

1 - Each time she flew back home, Rita would catch a cold because of the air conditioning.

2 - George went to bed but could not sleep because he now knew that there had been an accident.

3 - The sun shone into the room, which still smelled of the lamb chops Vera had cooked for lunch.

4 - Michael was a young man who, despite his age, had already made a fortune in real estate.

THE LAST WORD (continued)

Now try to answer the following questions.

What had Vera cooked?
- lamb
- beef
- fish

Write down the last words of each sentence:

Sentence #1: _____

Sentence #2: _____

Sentence #3: _____

Sentence #4: _____

Please check your answers against the previous page.

16

If you have not made any errors, you get one point.

THE ODD ONE OUT

This exercise tests your memory of general knowledge and trains your logical reasoning skills.

Find the odd word in the following series. Explain your answer.

usa.

Big Ben	British museum	Westminster	Rockefeller Center ✓	Tower bridge

The odd one is: _____

medical ✓

spade	scalpel	rake	pruning shears	trowel

The odd one is: _____

mollusk vs crustacean

snail ✓	crayfish	lobster	shrimp	crab

The odd one is: _____

PinkFlyod vs Manly

Diamonds	Two Girls from Little Rock	Bye Bye Baby	The Wall ✓	River of No Return

The odd one is: _____

F1 Pilot   Basketball

Michael Schumacher	Richard Hamilton	Tony Parker	Kevin Garnett	Paul Pierce

The odd one is: _____

17

If you have at least four correct answers, you get one point. ■

THE ODD ONE OUT

Find the odd word in the following series. Explain your answer.

star

| Sun ✓ | Mars | Mercury | Venus | Jupiter |

The odd one is: _____

actor

| D. H. Lawrence | F. Scott Fitzgerald | Oscar Wilde | Charles Dickens | Tom Cruise ✓ |

The odd one is: _____

Africa

| France | Morocco ✓ | Great Britain | Spain | Italy |

The odd one is: _____

fish

| beef | pork | cod ✓ | lamb | veal |

The odd one is: _____

Softwood.

| beech | oak | willow | fir ✓ | poplar |

The odd one is: _____

18

If you have at least four correct answers, you get one point. ■

TURNING AROUND

This exercise trains your visual acuity and, more specifically, your ability to mentally rotate an object.

> Determine whether the two figures below are identical or mirror images.

> If you get the correct answer, you get one point. ■

TURNING AROUND

Determine whether the two figures below are identical or mirror images.

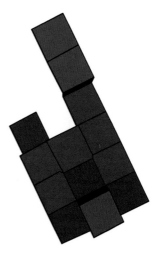

If you get the correct answer, you get one point. ▨

THIS STORY IS FULL OF BLANKS

In this set of exercises, you will analyze text and supply missing words by deduction and by drawing on your knowledge of grammar.

> Read the following text. Allow yourself three minutes to sup-
> ply the missing words from the list below. Each word may
> only be used once.

A thrilling character

Some _____ he had been a Russian spy, others that
he was _____ to one of Europe's _____ families.
Nearly all _____ acquaintances took _____ of
his incredible hospitality. _____ his castle, he gave
the _____ fabulous parties one _____ remember, and the most amazing thing of _____ is that
guests were never quite sure who the host _____. He
had also lived in the jungle for _____, and ornaments
in his home _____ tribute to the animal world he had
_____ there. You could _____ imagine what
amazing _____ this man was going to accomplish
next.

21

advantage	was	most	related	his
could	In	said	not	royal
all	paid	encountered	years	thing

> If you have found the right location for all words, you get one
> point. ▪

THIS STORY IS FULL OF BLANKS

> Read the following text. Allow yourself three minutes to supply the missing words from the list below. Each word may only be used once.

A horrid night

_____ professor James Blew was _____ sitting in his study when _____ urgent late night _____ call abruptly interrupted _____ from his reading. The elderly _____ of the university _____ disappeared for more than _____ days now, and the police phone _____ did not bring _____ news. They had found his _____ in a car _____ the Scotland castle where he usually liked to go during his _____ during the summer season. The police _____ would have to start _____

Oxford	Headmaster	two	him	near
soon	had	an	quietly	phone
investigation	weekends	good	body	call

> If you have found the right location for all words, you get one point. ▥

MOVING CHARACTERS

This set of exercises will help fine-tune your concentration and visual analysis skills. For this analysis you have to recognize characters and analyze their locations in space.

Take a careful look at the shape and location of the first series of hieroglyphics. In the second series, the characters have been moved and some have been replaced. Identify which characters have been replaced in the second series.

First series

23

Second series

If you have found which characters have been replaced, you get one point. ■

MOVING CHARACTERS

Take a careful look at the shape and location of the first series of hieroglyphics. In the second series, the characters have been moved and some have been replaced. Identify which characters have been replaced in the second series.

First series

24

Second series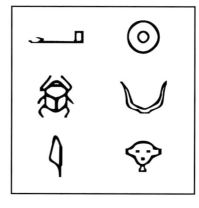

 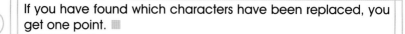

TIDY IT UP!

This exercise trains
- your ability to group items logically into various categories
- your memory of words
- your spatial memory
- your concentration

Classify the twenty items in this list in four categories and title each category.

AÏKIDO	WATERSKIING
BASKETBALL	LUGE
BOBSLED	SURFING
WAKEBOARDING	RUGBY
SOCCER	SAILING
HANDBALL -	SKIING
ICE HOCKEY	SNOWBOARDING
JUDO	TAE KWON DO
KARATE	WINDSURFING
THAI BOXING	VOLLEYBALL

25

Title:	Title:	Title:	Title:

If you have not made more than two mistakes, you get one point. ■

TIDY IT UP!

Classify the twenty items in this list in four categories and title each category.

HENRY JAMES
PINK FLOYD
DEBUSSY
BERLIOZ
THE BLACK EYED PEAS
J. M. BASQUIAT
JOHN IRVING
THE ROLLING STONES
NATHANIEL HAWTHORNE
SCHUBERT

LEONARDO DA VINCI
ANDY WARHOL
SALVADOR DALI
CHOPIN
TEXAS
F. SCOTT FITZGERALD
JAMES JOYCE
THE DOORS
LUCIAN FREUD
MOZART

Title:	Title:	Title:	Title:

If you have not made more than two mistakes, you get one point. ■

HURRAY FOR CHANGE

This exercise trains your mental flexibility and your strategy capacities, as well as concentration and visual and spatial acuity.

Link the following numbers and words by numerical order (from small to big) and alphabetical order, respectively. You cannot change your mind once you have traced a line nor link two elements twice. Start with the number marked "Begin" and end with the word marked "End."

Example: spring; 44; summer; 563; winter; 8152

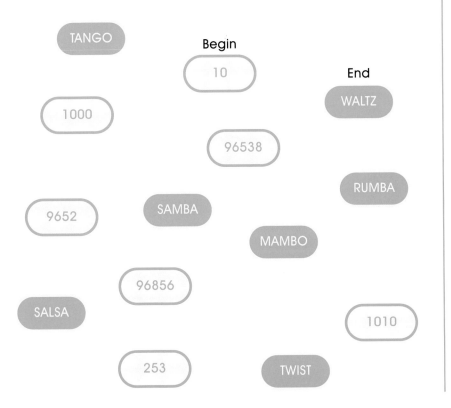

TANGO

Begin

10

End

WALTZ

27

1000

96538

RUMBA

9652

SAMBA

MAMBO

96856

SALSA

1010

253

TWIST

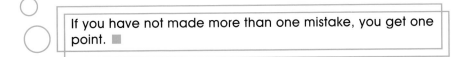

If you have not made more than one mistake, you get one point. ■

HURRAY FOR CHANGE

Link the following numbers and words by numerical order (from small to big) and alphabetical order, respectively. You cannot change your mind once you have traced a line nor link two elements twice. Start with the number marked "Begin" and end with the word marked "End."

Example: spring; 44; summer; 563; winter; 8152

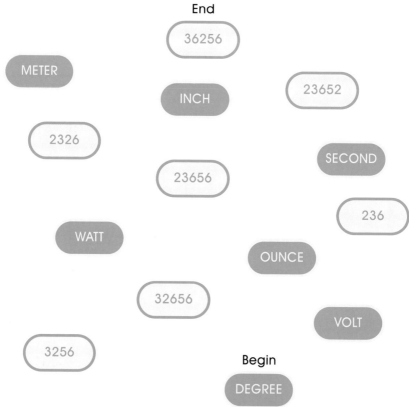

28

End

36256

METER

23652

INCH

2326

SECOND

23656

236

WATT

OUNCE

32656

VOLT

3256

Begin

DEGREE

If you have not made more than one mistake, you get one point. ■

THE RIGHT WORD

This exercise trains
- your memory of words (also called lexical memory)
- your understanding of sentences
- your spelling

> Find the word that corresponds to the definition.

1 - straight line segment that passes through the center of a circle or sphere and whose endpoints are on the circular boundary

diameter   radius   perimeter

2 - food made from flour, water, and sometimes eggs, which is mixed, kneaded, and formed into various shapes and boiled prior to consumption

doughnut   pasta   cake

3 - succession of rulers from the same family who maintain power for generations

decade   dynasty   genealogy

4 - individual writing instrument that applies ink to a surface, usually paper

pen   keyboard   screen

5 - view of an object or scene consisting of the outline filled in with a solid color interior

shadow   silhouette   profile

29

If you have not made any mistakes, you get one point. ▪

THE RIGHT WORD

Find the word that corresponds to the definition.

1 - Japanese word for comics and/or cartoons

manga kimono sari

2 - barrier across flowing water that obstructs, directs, or retards the flow, often creating a reservoir, lake, or impoundment

bridge dam viaduct

3 - strategic board game for two players, played on a square board of eight rows and eight columns

checkers dice chess

4 - medical disorder characterized by varying or persistent elevated blood-sugar levels, especially after eating

cancer illness diabetes

5 - small mammals sometimes affectionately known as bunnies

mice rabbits dogs

If you have not made any mistakes, you get one point. ▪

ENTANGLED FIGURES

This exercise will develop your ability to distinguish shapes when they are superimposed on each other.

Examine the figure below; then determine which three of the nine figures below it are combined to form the figure.

31

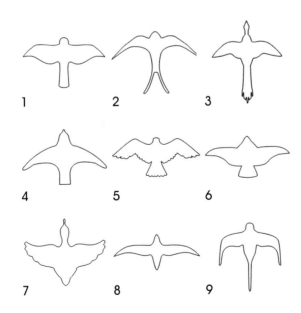

1

2

3

4

5

6

7

8

9

If you have found the three elements, you get one point. ▪

ENTANGLED FIGURES

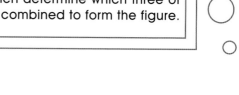

Examine the figure below; then determine which three of the nine figures below it are combined to form the figure.

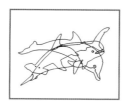

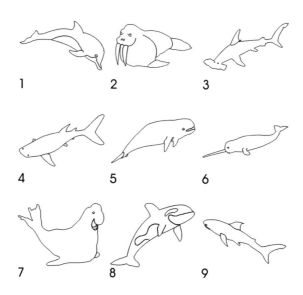

32

If you have found the three elements, you get one point. ▪

ELEPHANT'S MEMORY

This exercise is a challenging memory game. A good trick for memorizing a large number of items is to use a memorization strategy. To memorize the fifteen words below, group them by category. This will make it easier to recall them later.

Memorize the fifteen words in the grid below. Then turn the page to continue.

October	bean	sadness	cauliflower	January
compassion	pity	June	peas	joy
April	carrot	anger	December	lettuce

33

ELEPHANT'S MEMORY (continued)

Find the fifteen words you memorized from the previous page among the fifty words below.

joy	car	jacket	oak	sadness
red	pity	fly	radius	January
beech	bone	teacher	bean	violet
June	skirt	October	flower	sweater
leg	lettuce	bee	plane	carrot
compassion	green	anger	hand	poplar
train	cauliflower	shirt	butcher	blue
frog	peas	ant	truck	bank
December	yellow	fist	boat	April
hut	bookshop	rabbit	louse	trousers

Please check the answers against the previous page.

If you have found at least ten words out of the fifteen words, you get one point.

ELEPHANT'S MEMORY

Memorize the fifteen words in the grid below. Then turn the page to continue.

minute	sergeant	ring	week	officer
captain	necklace	second	general	month
earring	admiral	bracelet	hour	gem

ELEPHANT'S MEMORY (continued)

Find the fifteen words you memorized from the previous page among the fifty words below.

captain	second	pencil	wool	window
region	chill	sergeant	dollar	lake
cover	hour	ear	general	pan
marker	guitar	gem	finger	month
necklace	earring	pen	store	silk
harp	rice	euro	week	taste
paint	mayor	bracelet	view	landscape
cotton	ring	flute	minute	tattoo
corn	admiral	eyes	nose	cow
officer	bear	piano	country	mountain

Please check the answers against previous page.

If you have found at least ten words out of the fifteen words, you get one point.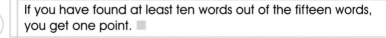

WHERE IS THE ODD ONE?

This exercise trains your
- visual and spatial acuity
- attention
- ability to resist interfering elements
- shape recognition ability

Find the odd one hidden in each series.

The odd one is ǝ

ӨӨӨӨӨӨӨӨӨӨӨӨӨӨӨӨӨӨӨӨӨӨӨӨӨӨӨӨӨӨӨӨӨӨӨӨӨӨ
ӨӨӨӨӨӨӨӨӨӨӨӨӨӨӨӨӨӨӨӨӨӨӨӨӨӨӨӨӨӨӨӨӨӨӨӨ
ӨӨӨӨӨӨӨӨӨӨӨӨӨӨӨӨӨӨӨӨӨӨӨӨӨӨӨӨӨӨӨӨӨӨӨӨ
ӨӨӨӨӨӨӨӨӨӨӨӨӨӨӨӨӨӨӨӨӨӨӨӨӨӨӨӨӨӨӨӨӨӨӨӨ
ӨӘӨӨӨӨӨӨӨӨӨӨӨӨӨӨӨӨӨӨӨӨӨӨӨӨӨӨӨӨӨӨӨӨӨӨ

The odd one is ⊙

◉◉◉◉◉◉◉◉◉◉◉◉◉◉◉◉◉◉◉◉◉◉◉◉◉◉◉◉◉◉◉◉◉◉◉◉
◉◉◉◉◉◉◉◉◉◉◉◉◉◉◉◉◉◉◉◉◉◉◉◉◉◉◉◉◉◉◉◉◉◉◉◉
◉◉◉⊙◉◉◉◉◉◉◉◉◉◉◉◉◉◉◉◉◉◉◉◉◉◉◉◉◉◉◉◉◉◉◉◉
◉◉◉◉◉◉◉◉◉◉◉◉◉◉◉◉◉◉◉◉◉◉◉◉◉◉◉◉◉◉◉◉◉◉◉◉
◉◉◉◉◉◉◉◉◉◉◉◉◉◉◉◉◉◉◉◉◉◉◉◉◉◉◉◉◉◉◉◉◉◉◉◉

The odd one is ♀

The odd one is ←

If you have found at least three out of the four odd ones, you get one point.

WHERE IS THE ODD ONE?

Find the odd one hidden in each series.

The odd one is }
{{
{{
{{
{{{}{{
{{{

The odd one is

The odd one is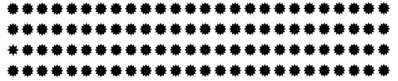

The odd one is *

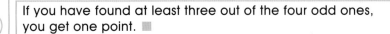

If you have found at least three out of the four odd ones, you get one point.

38

SPELLING MISTAKES

This exercise trains your memory of words and language (semantic memory). It sharpens your knowledge of English and trains your visual acuity.

Find the correct spelling of each word among three different options.

constitutional	constitussionnal	constitutionnal
harmonie	harmmony	harmony
comedie	comedy	commedy
millionnaire	millonaire	millionaire
obsolete	obsolette	obsolite
armamment	armament	armmement
literaly	literrally	literally
multiplicity	multiplisity	multipplicity
curently	currently	currentlly
elephant	ellephant	elefant
sustainnability	sustainabillity	sustainability
cowardisse	cowardice	kowardice
athmosphere	atemosphere	atmosphere
furniture	ferniture	furnitture

39

If you have found at least ten right answers, you get one point. ■

SPELLING MISTAKES

Find the correct spelling of each word among three different options.

stroberry	strawberry	strawbery
impresive	impressive	imppressive
loyallty	loyaltty	loyalty
exppression	expresion	expression
parallel	paralel	parrallel
medecine	medicine	midicine
eligibility	elligibility	eligibillity
miniatture	minniature	miniature
therrapist	therappist	therapist
philosophie	phillosophy	philosophy
disagreement	disagrement	disagreemment
humilliation	humiliation	hummiliation
powerfully	powerfuly	powerffully
orchestra	orrchestra	orkestra

40

If you have found at least ten right answers, you get one point. ▦

WRITING IN THE STARS

This exercise trains your logical reasoning capacity. It also calls upon your working memory.

Of the nine words in each list below, only six can be placed in the star. Arrows indicate the direction in which each word is placed. To assist you, one letter has already been placed in each star.

EXHAUST
CONTACT
COTTAGE
TRACHEA
SPATULA
TETANUS
WATTAGE
SUCCESS
EYEBROW

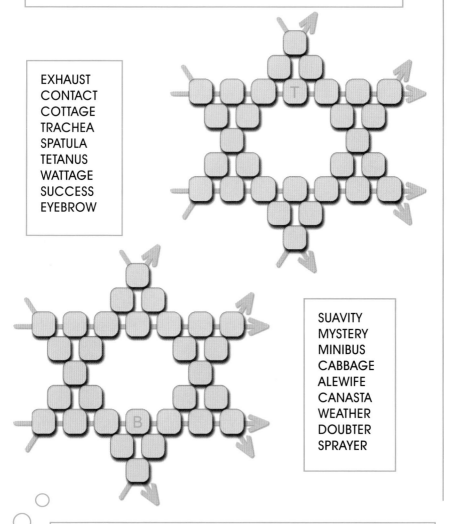

SUAVITY
MYSTERY
MINIBUS
CABBAGE
ALEWIFE
CANASTA
WEATHER
DOUBTER
SPRAYER

41

If you correctly filled in the two stars, you get one point. ■

WRITING IN THE STARS

Of the nine words in each list below, only six can be placed in the star. Arrows indicate the direction in which each word is placed. To assist you, one letter has already been placed in each star.

CORONER
RELAPSE
REVERIE
HEROINE
HEATHER
SCHOLAR
WHISPER
SPARROW
INVOICE

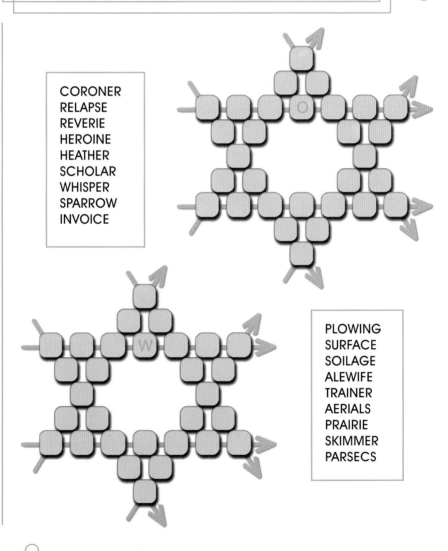

PLOWING
SURFACE
SOILAGE
ALEWIFE
TRAINER
AERIALS
PRAIRIE
SKIMMER
PARSECS

42

If you correctly filled in the two stars, you get one point. ■

OBJECTS, WHERE ARE YOU?

This exercise trains your capacity to create a link between two pieces of different information: the shape of a picture and its location. Creating these links makes memorization easier. A good visual acuity and a high level of focus are also required.

> Take a careful look at the shape and location of the six items in this grid. Then turn the page to continue.

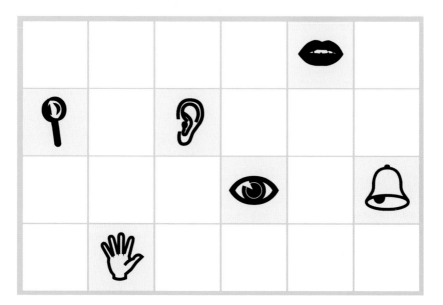

43

OBJECTS, WHERE ARE YOU? (continued)

Place each of the six pictures from the preceding page in the correct yellow rectangles below.

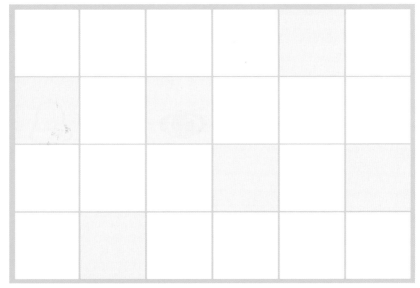

Please check your answers against the previous page.

If you have not made more than one mistake, you get one point. ■

OBJECTS, WHERE ARE YOU?

Take a careful look at the shape and location of the six items in this grid. Then turn the page to continue.

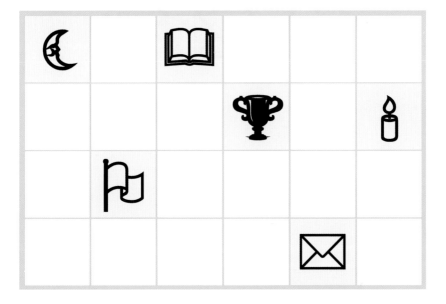

45

OBJECTS, WHERE ARE YOU? (continued)

Place each of the six pictures from the preceding page in the correct yellow rectangles below.

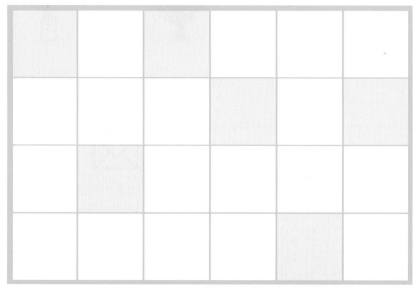

Please check your answers against the previous page.

If you have not made more than one mistake, you get one point. ■

MOSAICS

This exercise trains
- spatial exploration
- mental imagery
- visual concentration

Take a careful look at the four elements below and try to determine which ones are not part of the figure below. Beware, some pictures might just have been turned around!

1   2   3   4

47

If you have not made any errors, you get one point. ■

MOSAICS

Take a careful look at the four elements below and try to determine which ones are not part of the figure below. Beware, some pictures might just have been turned around!

1

2

3

4

48

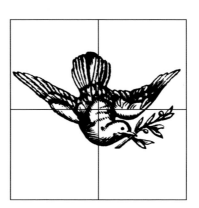

If you have not made any errors, you get one point. ∎

ANAGRAMS

This exercise trains your mental lexicon or vocabulary. It will also call on your reasoning capacities, as you will have to use your knowledge to determine words based on their first letters.

> The letters of the ten following words have been mixed up. They are all related to Cinema. The first letter of each word is given as a clue.

OOSTIGNH: S_____

MEACAR: C_____

CASTSRE: A_____

SITGNAC: C_____

MTOINAANI: A_____

TTLSBUISE: S_____

OGLAIDUE: D_____

OIRANESC: S_____

TROIDCRE: D_____

KCARUONSDT: S_____

> If you have found at least eight words, you get one point. ▥

ANAGRAMS

The letters of the ten following words have been mixed up. They are all related to Weather. The first letter of each word is given as a clue.

REOFACST: F_____

MUTREAREEPT: T_____

AFHERNHTIE: F_____

MSOPEAHRET: A_____

IAELCMT: C_____

HGTUISNL: S_____

ODTROAN: T_____

RRUHIANCE: H_____

TSEEITLAL: S_____

RTROABMEE: B_____

If you have found at least eight words, you get one point. ▧

BASKETBALL IN NEW YORK

This exercise trains your problem-solving capacities by training you how to create strategies that take into account your starting point and the goal you want to reach. For this exercise, you will need to create goals and subgoals and use mental imagery.

Determine the minimal number of moves needed to move from the configuration in Figure A to the configuration of Figure B. Follow these rules:
- balls may only move out of baskets upwards
- you may not place more than three balls in one basket
- you may only move one ball at a time

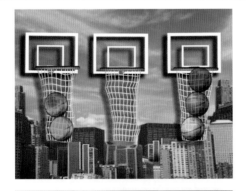

A

B

If you have found the fewest number of moves necessary, you get one point. ■

BASKETBALL IN NEW YORK

Determine the minimal number of moves needed to move from the configuration in Figure A to the configuration of Figure B. Follow these rules:
- balls may only move out of baskets upwards
- you may not place more than three balls in one basket
- you may only move one ball at a time

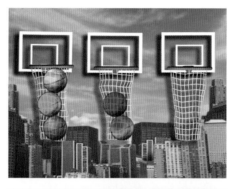

A

B

If you have found the fewest number of moves necessary, you get one point. ■

WHAT IS THE RECIPE?

This exercise trains your memory and also your concentration in the kitchen! Reading a recipe is the intermediary step between learning a new task and retrieving memorized information. This exercise requires you to use your memory and concentration resources.

Memorize the list of ingredients from the recipe below. You should memorize both the ingredients and their quantity. Then read the recipe carefully (you do not have to memorize it, but it might be useful!). Then turn the page.

GREEK YOGURT DIP

Ingredients

- 16 oz. (455 g.) strained yogurt
- 1 cucumber
- 4 garlic cloves
- salt
- oil
- vinegar

Preparation

Grate the garlic and mix it with salt and vinegar.
Peel the cucumber, grate it, and squeeze it until all its water is
    removed.
Put the yogurt into a bowl and add the cucumber to it.
Then mix the yogurt with the mixture of grated garlic.
Stir the contents until all the ingredients are well mixed.
Add some oil.
Serve chilled or at room temperature.

53

WHAT IS THE RECIPE? (continued)

Find all the ingredients for the recipe on the previous page from among the twenty ingredients below. Strike through the ingredients that were not part of the recipe. Where applicable, write the quantity beside the ingredient.

vinegar _____

oil _____

fish _____

butter _____

whipped cream _____

milk _____

potatoes _____

tomatoes _____

beans _____

cucumber _____

rice _____

strained yogurt _____

bread _____

flour _____

grated cheese_____

pepper _____

garlic _____

salt _____

thyme_____

coriander _____

Please check your answers against the previous page.

If you have not made more than two mistakes, you get one point. ▪

WHAT IS THE RECIPE?

Memorize the list of ingredients from the recipe below. You should memorize both the ingredients and their quantity. Then read the recipe carefully (you do not have to memorize it, but it might be useful!). Then turn the page.

CLASSIC CHOCOLATE TRUFFLES

Ingredients

- 28 oz. (800 g.) good-quality bittersweet chocolate
- 1 cup (250 ml.) cream
- 1/4 cup (62.5 ml.) chocolate liqueur
- Powdered sugar
- Good-quality cocoa

Preparation

Chop 12 ounces of chocolate into chunks. Place chocolate pieces in a food processor with a metal blade and process until the chocolate is finely chopped. Bring cream to a boil. With food processor running, add cream to chocolate and process until cream is completely incorporated. With processor still running, add liqueur and process until incorporated. Refrigerate chocolate mixture until chilled.

Using powdered sugar on your hands to prevent the chocolate from sticking, roll teaspoonsful of the chocolate mixture into balls. Refrigerate again until chilled.

Melt 16 ounces of chocolate in the top of a double boiler. Allow chocolate to cool to about 90 degrees F. Take each chocolate ball and dip it in the melted chocolate. Place the chocolate ball in the cocoa to coat.

Refrigerate once again.

Store truffles in the refrigerator until one hour before serving.

55

WHAT IS THE RECIPE?

Find all the ingredients for the recipe on the previous page from among the twenty ingredients below. Strike through the ingredients that were not part of the recipe. Where applicable, write the quantity beside the ingredient.

caramel _____

chopped nuts _____

sugar _____

margarine _____

soy milk _____

honey _____

butter _____

vanilla extract _____

cream _____

flour _____

eggs _____

bitter sweet chocolate _____

egg yolks _____

chopped pecan _____

baking powder _____

liqueur _____

cocoa _____

grated coconut _____

cinnamon _____

chocolate chips _____

Please check your answers against the previous page.

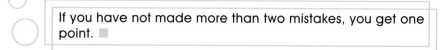

If you have not made more than two mistakes, you get one point. ■

WHAT IS THE DIFFERENCE?

This exercise trains your visual acuity.

Identify six differences between these two pictures.

If you have identified the six differences, you get one point. ▓

WHAT IS THE DIFFERENCE?

Identify six differences between these two pictures.

If you have identified the six differences, you get one point. ▥

POINTS OF VIEW

This exercise trains your visual and spatial skills. Imagine that you are observing the landscape firsthand. Use your visual and spatial skills to establish relationships between elements in the landscape and to coordinate various points of view.

> Take a careful look at the location of the five objects in this landscape.

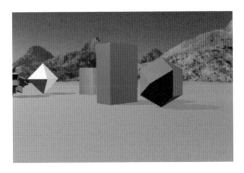

59

The image below shows the same landscape as seen from above. Determine as fast as possible where you would stand in the scenery to view the landscape as it appears in the top image.

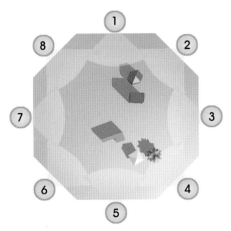

> If you have found the correct answer, you get one point. ■

POINTS OF VIEW

Take a careful look at the location of the five objects in this landscape.

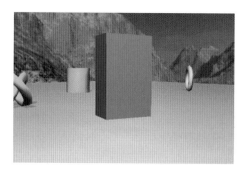

The image below shows the same landscape as seen from above. Determine as fast as possible where you would stand in the scenery to view the landscape as it appears in the top image.

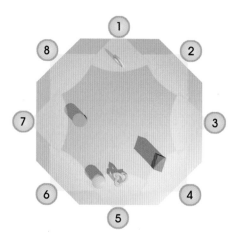

If you have found the correct answer, you get one point. ■

THE MYSTERY WORD

This exercise trains several abilities simultaneously:
- your ability to make pairs by associating vowels and consonants
- fast visual exploration
- semantic memory (memory of words)

Find a seven-letter word in the grids below. The first two letters of each word are in color.

D	G	N	S
O	S	I	T
T	T	L	Y
N	E	D	I

C	S	M	A
F	U	R	L
S	R	E	L
B	R	I	I

T	E	F	H
O	U	D	L
R	R	I	E
A	I	S	M

G	T	I	P
U	I	H	J
R	T	S	A
E	Y	E	L

If you have found the four words, you get one point. ■

THE MYSTERY WORD

Find an eight-letter word in the grids below. The first two letters of each word are in color.

E	Y	T	I
R	L	U	R
Y	M	C	E
C	I	B	S

B	P	P	E
U	R	O	R
L	D	I	T
M	I	V	Y

D	S	I	M
L	T	O	M
R	U	N	S
E	U	E	I

S	E	C	B
S	S	N	L
D	R	I	O
E	P	T	U

If you have found the four words, you get one point.

SHAPES AND COLORS

This exercise trains your concentration capacities as well as your ability to remember geometrical shapes.

> **Memorize the four figures below. Then turn the page.**

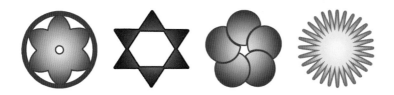

63

SHAPES AND COLORS (continued)

Now try to find the four figures you memorized from among the sixteen figures displayed below. As a hint, there is one correct figure per line.

64

Please check your answers against the previous page.

If you have found at least three correct figures, you get one point. ▪

SHAPES AND COLORS

Memorize the four figures below. Then turn the page.

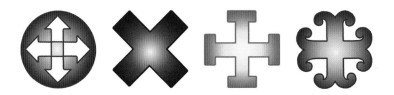

SHAPES AND COLORS (continued)

Now try to find the four figures you memorized from among the sixteen figures displayed below. As a hint, there is one correct figure per line.

66

Please check your answers against the previous page.

If you have found at least three correct figures, you get one point. ■

DECIPHER

This exercise will draw upon your concentration, language, and logic skills to decipher a quotation whose letters have been replaced by symbols.

> Try to decipher this quotation. Letters are always replaced by the same symbol. The blue symbols are consonants; the red ones are vowels.

Replace the picture below with a well-known quotation.

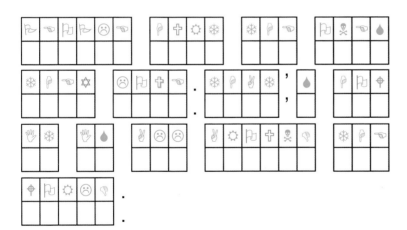

67

If you have deciphered the quotation, you get one point. ■

DECIPHER

Try to decipher this quotation. Letters are always replaced by the same symbol. The blue symbols are consonants; the red ones are vowels.

Replace the picture below with a well-known quotation.

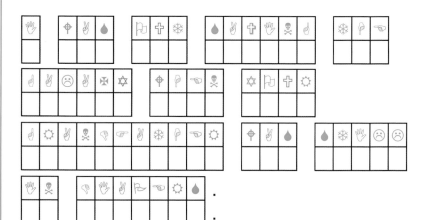

Replace the picture below with a well-known quotation.

If you have deciphered the quotation, you get one point. ■

PLAY ON WORDS

This exercise trains your semantic memory (memory of words) and calls upon your vocabulary.

> Find the antonym (opposite) of each word. The first letter is given as a hint.

beautiful: u_gly_

rich: p_oor_

close: o_pen_

long: s_hort_

discreet: i_ndescreet_

forbidden: a_llowed_

true: f_alse_

accept: r_eject_

admirable: d_ispisable_

quiet: l_oud_

> Find which word cannot be a synonym of the four others in each row.

weird	uncanny	problematic	strange	unusual

consider	reflect on	ponder	think	tell

manufacture	make	create	produce	meditate

take off	gain	take in	earn	pull in

> If you have not made more than two mistakes, you get one point.

PLAY ON WORDS

Find the antonym (opposite) of each word. The first letter is given as a hint.

small: b_ig_____   careful: c_areless_____
raw: c_ooked_____   increasing: d_ecreasing_____
complicate: s_implify_____   empty: f_ull_____
busy: i_dle_____   less: m_ore_____
easy: h_ard_____   few: m_any_____

70

Find which word cannot be a synonym of the four others in each row.

celebrated	famed	famous	renowned	tranquil

elastic	rigid	flexible	pliable	pliant

fate	pride	destiny	fortune	luck

relativity	understand-ing	sympathy	comprehen-sion	agreement

If you have not made more than two mistakes, you get one point. ▦

WHO AM I?

This exercise calls upon your general knowledge.

Whose life is described below?

I was born in Peoria, Illinois, in 1921. After graduating summa cum laude from Smith in 1942, I was awarded scholarships to work toward a doctorate in psychology but chose to decline. I married in 1947 and for nearly 20 years lived the life of a conventional suburban housewife and mother. I had three children before getting divorced in 1969.

Spurred by my own dissatisfaction as a housewife, I began a series of feminist studies in 1957. These studies became the basis for my controversial exposé of women's traditional roles in modern industrial societies, a landmark work published in 1963. The critique became an international bestseller and is credited with generating the so-called second wave of modern feminism. In 1966 I co-founded the National Organization for Women (NOW) and served as its first president (1966–70).

71

I am _____

If you have found the correct answer, you get one point.

WHO AM I?

Whose life is described below?

I was born in London, England, on February 27, 1932, where I lived for the first seven years of my life. In 1939, my family relocated to Los Angeles, California. Already a beauty at a young age, I was taken for a screen test that impressed the Universal Pictures executives enough to sign a contract with me. My first of many films to come, *There's One Born Every Minute*, was released when I was ten years old. Universal dropped my contract after that film, but I was soon picked up by MGM.

My performance in a 1944 smash hit in which I played opposite Mickey Rooney launched me as a child star. Throughout the 1940s and into the early 1950s, I appeared in film after film. By 1956 when I appeared in the hit *Giant* with James Dean, I had grown into a beautiful young woman.

In 1960, I won my first Academy Award for my performance as call girl Gloria Wandrous. In 1963, I starred in one of the most expensive productions of the time, earning an unprecedented salary of $1,000,000. I won my second Oscar in 1966 for my performance as Martha in *Who's Afraid of Virginia Woolf?*

I am _____

If you have found the correct answer, you get one point.

SLEIGHT OF HAND

This exercise trains your attention capacities and requires a good level of mental imagery that is very useful in daily life.

> Among the six hands below, find the right hands and the left hands.

1

2

3

4

5

6

73

> Among the six hands below, find the right hands and the left hands.

1

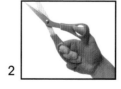
2

3

4

5

6

> If you have not made more than one mistake, you get one point. ▦

SLEIGHT OF HAND

Among the six hands below, find the right hands and the left hands.

1

2

3

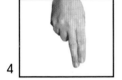
4

5

6

74

Among the six hands below, find the right hands and the left hands.

1

2

3

4

5

6

If you have not made more than one mistake, you get one point. ▪

NO PROBLEM!

This exercise trains your logical and reasoning capacities, as well as your working memory.

> Try to solve these two mathematical problems in your head.

Problem #1

To create costumes for a play, a costume director buys:

- 25 thread spools of 10 feet each,
- 30 ribbons of 100 inches each,
- 7 wool balls of 7 feet each

What is the total length of these elements?

Problem #2

The size of a particular algae doubles every day. Knowing it will take 40 days for the algae to cover the surface of a pool, how many days will it need to cover 1/4 of the pool?

> If you have found at least one out of the two solutions, you get one point. ■

NO PROBLEM!

Try to solve these two mathematical problems in your head.

Problem #1

Miss Smith would like to buy a car. The first car dealer she meets shows her a $25,000 model and offers Miss Smith a 5% discount if she buys the car immediately. Another car seller shows her a $22,000 model with a 4% discount.

Which dealer offers the bigger discount?

_____

With the discount, which vehicle is less expensive?

_____

Problem #2

Mr. Martin counts his jam jars. All the jars except three contain apricots; all the jars except three contain prunes; all the jars except three contain raspberries; all the jars except three contain cherries.

How many jam jars does Mr Martin have?

_____

If you have found at least one solution out of two, you get one point. ■

FIND YOUR WAY

This exercise trains your attention specifically for spatial information. It trains your visual and spatial memory, too.

> Take a careful look at the figure below, paying special attention to the directional arrows that connect the seven colored circles. Try to memorize the order in which the arrows progress from beginning to end. Then turn the page.

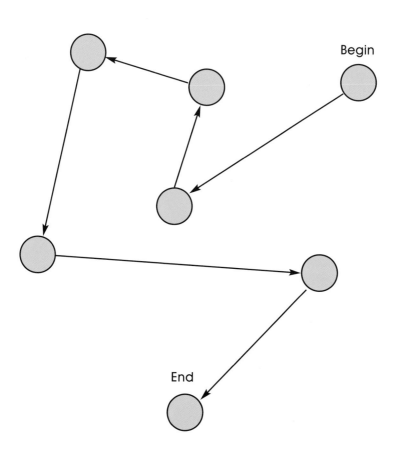

Begin

End

FIND YOUR WAY (continued)

Reconstruct the figure from the previous page by drawing the connecting arrows.

Begin

Please check your answer against the previous page.

If you have not made more than one mistake, you get one point. ■

FIND YOUR WAY

Take a careful look at the figure below, paying special attention to the directional arrows that connect the seven colored circles. Try to memorize the order in which the arrows progress from beginning to end. Then turn the page.

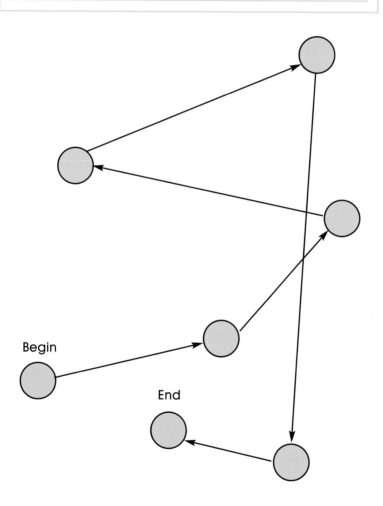

Begin

End

FIND YOUR WAY (continued)

> Reconstruct the figure from the previous page by drawing the connecting arrows.

Begin

Please check your answer against the previous page.

> If you have not made more than one mistake, you get one point. ▪

Comments on scores for level #1

COMMENTS level #1

CALCULATE YOUR RESULTS

Write down the number of points obtained at level #1:

Number of ▨	Number of ▥	Number of ▤	Number of ▥	Number of ▦	TOTAL

COMMENTS ON YOUR SCORE

If you earned 0 to 21 points:
Perhaps these exercises were completely foreign to you or you were not sufficiently focused on them. Whatever the reason, there is plenty of room for progress. Try to really focus now, because the 2nd level is even more difficult!

If you earned 22 to 43 points:
Good job. You've done fairly well at this level. You may have found some exercises harder than others, but on a global level, your neurons are quite good. Now that you have had a bit of practice, you will probably be able to get amazing results at the next level.

If you earned 44 to 64 points:
Wow, these are obviously very fit neurons! Indeed, your score is excellent for this first round. Keep up the good work! The next series should not be a problem for you!

COMMENTS level#1

COMMENTS BY COGNITIVE AREA

Memory score ■

If you earned 0 to 6 points:

Practice makes perfect. The more you train, the stronger your memory will be. Make an effort, as memory is constantly needed in daily life . . . and training is just the right thing to do!

If you earned 7 to 13 points:

Your score is good, but you may experience certain gaps in your memory that are probably due more to a lack of attention than true memory loss. With a little more training, you'll be on your way to having a great memory.

If you earned 14 to 20 points:

Birthdays, shopping lists, or poems known by heart are probably not a problem for you! Your memory is very good. Your challenge now is to do as well at a higher level.

Language score ▥

If you earned 0 to 4 points:

Crosswords or word games are just so boring? Maybe it's time you changed your mind! Training and using words is the only way to improve your language skills.

If you earned 5 to 9 points:

You may not be a language champ, but you've earned a pretty good score. There is no secret to improving: just train more. You may then realize that playing with language is easier than you thought.

If you earned 10 to 14 points:

Grammar, spelling, vocabulary, and language have no secrets for you. According to your results, your command of the English language is excellent! Let's just see what you get at the next level.

COMMENTS level #1

Attention and concentration score ■

If you earned 0 to 2 points:

It looks like you are easily distracted. Be sure you find a quiet place to concentrate on level #2.

If you earned 3 to 5 points:

Your score shows that your attention capacities are high, but maybe you find it hard to stay focused for long periods of time. With more training, you can learn to resist distractions.

If you earned 6 to 8 points:

Excellent score! That's great news, because attention and concentration are required for all the exercises of the book. Try to remain as focused for the next level.

Logical reasoning score ■

If you earned 0 to 3 points:

Logic, hypotheses, and deductive reasoning quite obviously are not your cup of tea. Even if you find these exercises tedious, don't neglect them! Logical reasoning is constantly called upon in daily life.

If you earned 4 to 8 points:

Even if logical reasoning is not one of your favorite activities, you seem to have a knack for it. Training can certainly help you improve your score.

If you earned 9 to 12 points:

You are a fan of logic and reasoning and you know perfectly well how to carry out logical reasoning processes to achieve your goals. Your score is great on this first part. Let's see how you do with the second series of exercises.

COMMENTS level 1

Visual and spatial score ▦

If you earned 0 to 3 points:

Mental rotation and orientation do not come naturally for everyone and perhaps they are not your strong suit. However, these skills are essential in our 3D world, and a little more training will make you stronger.

If you earned 4 to 6 points:

Good job! It is not so easy to locate oneself in space and carry out mental rotations, and you have achieved this quite well. Now that you are familiar with the exercises, you can test yourself with the harder level!

If you earned 7 to 10 points:

You are a pro at situating yourself in space and navigating your 3D world! Your high score indicates your strong abilities in the visual and spatial fields. Keep up the good work at the next level!

SECOND PART

Exercises: level #2

The solutions are on page 189.

RIGHT OR WRONG?

Decide whether the following statements are right or wrong.

1 - The true name of James Dean is James Francis Dean.

2 - **The** Patella is a knee bone.

3 - A wishbone boom is an accessory used in windsurfing.

4 - **The** Yalta conference occurred in 1944.

5 - There were four Brontë Sisters.

6 - Amethyst is a purple variety of quartz.

7 - The Norwegian flag is yellow and blue.

8 - *Moby Dick* is the story of a nice whale.

9 - The square root of 144 is 12.

10 - The National Geographic Society was founded in 1888.

11 - The Mississippi river flows along the western boundary of the state of Mississippi.

12 - Horses belong to the Bovidae family.

13 - The chemical symbol for Sodium is So.

14 - Leonardo di Caprio starred in *The Beach*.

15 - The carrot is a root vegetable.

16 - The Europeans first came in contact with the Iroquois in the 17th century.

17 - Mexican people speak Portuguese.

18 - Henry James wrote *What Maisie Knew*.

19 - Mozart was a classical music composer.

20 - Bats are reptiles.

You need at least ten right answers to get one point.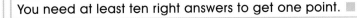

89

RIGHT OR WRONG?

Decide whether the following statements are right or wrong.

1 - Tea contains caffeine.

2 - *Wuthering Heights* was written by Emily Brontë.

3 - The Twist is a dance from the 1980s.

4 - Brass is a copper-zinc alloy.

5 - The word *totem* is of Native American origin.

6 - Harrison Ford acted in *Hook*.

7 - "Trapezium" is a word used for both a bone and a muscle.

8 - The painter J. M. Basquiat died in a car accident.

9 - Dolphins are fish.

10 - Writing verse uses meter.

11 - Bill Clinton was the 42nd president of the USA.

12 - Sushi is a Japanese specialty.

13 - Pope John Paul II was Romanian.

14 - Leonardo Da Vinci was Italian.

15 - The Bay of Pigs invasion occurred while Nixon was President.

16 - Nymphs are the young of certain insects.

17 - Lance Armstrong is a soccer player.

18 - The peso is the currency of Chile.

19 - Bill Gates was the founder and CEO of Microsoft.

20 - A hexagon has eight edges and vertices.

You need at least ten right answers to get one point.

ADJECTIVE OR NOUN?

This grid contains eight adjectives and eight nouns. Can you find them?

old	way	loneliness	clumsy
property	apple	weird	helium
broken	funny	big	furniture
mad	man	tired	honor

In this grid, classify the words as adjectives or nouns and write them down in alphabetical order.

91

Adjectives	Nouns

If you have not made more than three errors, you get one point. ■

ADJECTIVE OR NOUN?

This grid contains eight adjectives and eight nouns. Can you find them?

terrible	horrible	crazy	madness
certainty	charity	folly	kindness
evidence	horrid	certain	useless
pitiless	horror	pity	restless

In this grid, classify the words as adjectives or nouns and write them down in alphabetical order.

Adjectives	Nouns

If you have not made more than three errors, you get one point. ▓

TOWERS OF HANOI

Determine the fewest number of moves necessary to change the configuration in Figure A to that shown in Figure B. You must observe these rules:

- You may not place a larger disk on a smaller one.
- You may move only one disk at a time.

A

B

If you have found the fewest number of moves necessary, you get one point. ■

TOWERS OF HANOI

Determine the fewest number of moves necessary to change the configuration in Figure A to that shown in Figure B. You must observe these rules:

- You may not place a larger disk on a smaller one.
- You may move only one disk at a time.

A

B

If you have found the fewest number of moves necessary, you get one point. ■

CHIVALRY

Take a careful look at the shape, the colors, and the patterns of the shield below. Then turn the page to continue.

CHIVALRY (continued)

Select the various elements that make up the shield on the previous page.

Choose its shape:

1 2 3
4 5 6

Choose its colors:

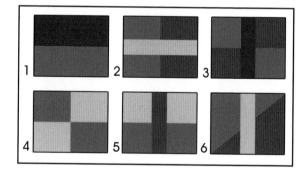

1 2 3
4 5 6

Choose its pattern:

1 2 3
4 5 6

If the shield is identical, you get one point. ◼

CHIVALRY

Take a careful look at the shape, the colors, and the patterns of the shield below. Then turn the page to continue.

CHIVALRY (continued)

Select the various elements that make up the shield on the previous page.

Choose its shape:

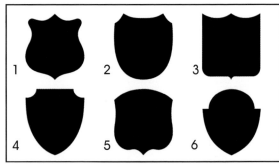

Choose its colors:

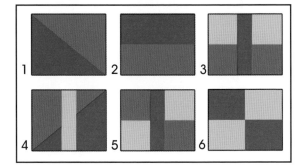

Choose its pattern:

If the shield is identical, you get one point. ▪

THE LAST WORD

> Carefully read the following six sentences and try to memorize the last word of each sentence. Then turn the page to continue.

1 - From the plane, they could see the gorgeous canyons and the Atlantic coast of the island.

2 - The first thing Carrie would do when she arrived at the office would be to get herself a cup of strong coffee.

3 - Each time Linda came back from one of her trips, she brought some great gifts for all the kids.

4 - Vince asked if they could hurry up a bit so that they would be home before nightfall.

5 - Geena was constantly on a diet and went to fitness classes in the evenings, with one of her best friends.

6 - Jack thought he could fix the car himself but unfortunately he did not have the right tools in his garage.

THE LAST WORD (continued)

Now try to answer the following questions.

What could they see from the plane?
- — - canyons
- lakes
- mountains

What did Vince ask?
- to slow down
- to sing
- — - to hurry up

Write down the last words of each sentence:

Sentence #1: _____ IsC _____

Sentence #2: _____ Cor _____

Sentence #3: _____ Kids _____

Sentence #4: _____ quichtf _____

Sentence #5: _____ friends _____

Sentence #6: _____ Hurry _____

Please check your answers against the previous page.

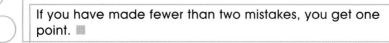

If you have made fewer than two mistakes, you get one point. ▦

THE LAST WORD

Carefully read the following six sentences and try to memorize the last word of each sentence. Then turn the page to continue.

1 - The visit to the castle was cancelled because rain fell constantly for four days.

2 - Last night James went to say hello to his great aunt and was quite surprised to find there was nobody home.

3 - Before each climb, mountaineering guides advised everyone on how to avoid creating an avalanche.

4 - While in the Greek islands, Joseph learned how to dance the local dance, which included wearing a skirt.

5 - The priest did not know what to do to draw their attention to the disastrous state of the roof.

6 - For the first time, David won a medal during a horse-jumping competition.

THE LAST WORD (continued)

Now try to answer the following questions.

What did David win?
- a trophy
- a medal
- a cup

What prevented the visit to the castle?
- rain
- snow
- fog

Write down the last words of each sentence:

Sentence #1: _____ R. _____

Sentence #2: _____ homd _____

Sentence #3: _____ gwal _____

Sentence #4: _____ Skif _____

Sentence #5: _____ Lud _____

Sentence #6: _____ Comp _____

Please check your answers against the previous page.

If you have made fewer than two mistakes, you get one point.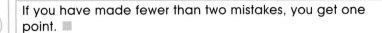

THE ODD ONE OUT

Find the odd word in the following series. Explain your answer.

Houston	Miami	Montreal	Seattle	Washington

can

The odd one is: _____

Celsius	Fahrenheit	Faraday	Newton	Kelvin

The odd one is: _____

american vs British

Eurythmics	Journey	Depeche Mode	The Police	Dire Straits

The odd one is: _____

explorer vs painter

Marco Polo	Jacques Cartier	Vasco de Gama	James Cook	Raffaello

The odd one is: _____

hat vs shoes

stetson	ballerina slipper	high-heel	boots	mocassin

The odd one is: _____

If you have at least three right answers, you get one point. ■

THE ODD ONE OUT

Find the odd word in the following series. Explain your answer.

tree

bolette	eucalyptus	morel	chanterelle	truffle

The odd one is: _____

not Woody

Everyone Says I Love You	Mighty Aphrodite	Annie Hall	The Godfather	Match Point

The odd one is: _____

Spanish leader

Churchill	Franco	Thatcher	Blair	Wilson

The odd one is: _____

Strmg vs wind

violin	tuba	horn	saxophone	trumpet

The odd one is: _____

freshwater   _salt_

trout	herring	shark	ray	tuna

The odd one is: _____

If you have at least three right answers, you get one point. ▪

TURNING AROUND

Two of the figures below are identical and one is a mirror image. Determine which is the mirror image.

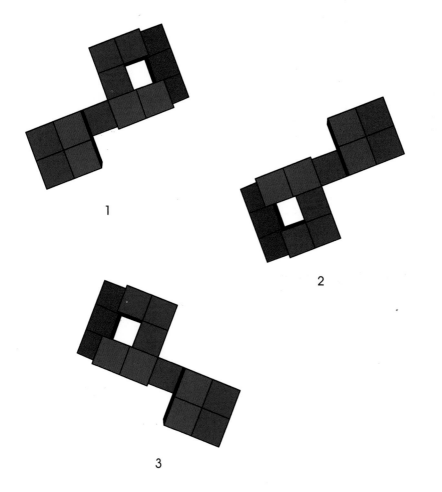

1

2

3

105

TURNING AROUND

Two of the figures below are identical and one is a mirror image. Determine which is the mirror image.

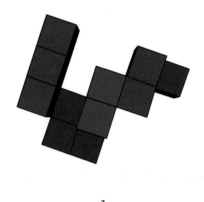

1

2

3

If you find the right answer, you get one point. ▨

THIS STORY IS FULL OF BLANKS

> Read the following paragraph and then try to complete it in fewer than three minutes with the fifteen words available. Each word may only be used once. The paragraph is an excerpt from classical literature.

From Sherwood Anderson's *Winesburg, Ohio*

During the _____ year of young David's _____, he saw his mother but _____, and she became for _____ just a woman with _____ he had once _____. Still he could not get _____ figure out of his mind _____ as he grew _____ it became more definite. When he was _____ years old he went _____ the Bentley farm to _____. Old Jesse came into _____ and fairly _____ that he be given charge of _____ boy.

last	older	her	and	seldom
the	lived	boyhood	him	whom
town	live	demanded	twelve	to

> If you have not made more than two mistakes, you get one point. ▦

THIS STORY IS FULL OF BLANKS

> Read the following paragraph and then try to complete it in fewer than three minutes with the fifteen words available. Each word may only be used once. The paragraph is an excerpt from classical literature.

From Malcom Lowry's *Under the Volcano*

But the doctor could not of _course_ come to Tomalin with them, though this was never _all_, since just then the conversation was _not_ interrupted by a sudden terrific detonation, that _shook_ the house and sent birds skimming panic-stricken _____ over the garden. Target _____ in the Sierra Madre. The Consul had _been_ half aware of it in his sleep earlier. _Puffs_ of smoke went _drifting_ high over the rocks below Popo at the end of the valley. Three _black_ vultures came tearing through the trees _low_ over the roof with soft _hoarse_ cries like the cries of love. Driven at _____ speed by their fear they _seemed_ almost to capsize, keeping close _____, but balancing at different angles to avoid collision.

practice	been	Puffs	shook	black
seemed	discussed	all	low	violently
course	together	hoarse	drifting	unaccus-tomed

> If you have not made more than two mistakes, you get one point. ■

MOVING CHARACTERS

Take a careful look at the shape and location of the first series of hieroglyphics. In the second series, the characters have been moved and some have been replaced. Identify which characters have been replaced in the second series.

First series

Second series

If you have not made more than one mistake, you get one point. ▦

MOVING CHARACTERS

Take a careful look at the shape and location of the first series of hieroglyphics. In the second series, the characters have been moved and some have been replaced. Identify which characters have been replaced in the second series.

First series

Second series

If you have not made more than one mistake, you get one point. ▧

TIDY IT UP!

Classify the twenty items in this list in four categories and title each category.

MICHIGAN
CASPIAN
RED
CHINA
PACIFIC
AMAZON
INDIAN
ARCTIC
VICTORIA
NESS

BAIKAL
MEDITERRANEAN
MISSISSIPPI
NILE
BERING
THAMES
ATLANTIC
AMUR
SOUTHERN
GREAT SALT

111

Title: LAKE	Title: River	Title: OCEANS	Title: SEA

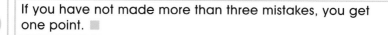
If you have not made more than three mistakes, you get one point. ■

TIDY IT UP!

Classify the twenty items in this list in four categories and title each category.

KILOGRAM	PINT
INCH	QUART
HOUR	YARD
NANOSECOND	MILE
FLUID OUNCE	MINUTE
OUNCE	TON
STONE	POUND
METER	GALLON
FEET	LITER
MILLISECOND	SECOND

Title: MET	Title: Time	Title: British	Title:

If you have not made more than two mistakes, you get one point.

HURRAY FOR CHANGE

Link the following numbers and words by numerical order (from small to big) and alphabetical order, respectively. You cannot change your mind once you have traced a line nor link two elements twice. Start with the number marked "Begin" and end with the word marked "End."

Example: bear; algae; dog; lichen; mouse; fungi

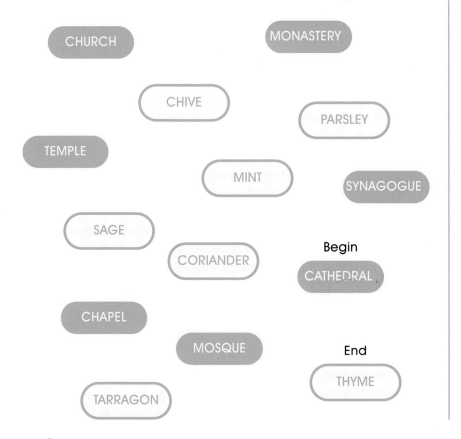

CHURCH

MONASTERY

CHIVE

PARSLEY

113

TEMPLE

MINT

SYNAGOGUE

SAGE

Begin

CORIANDER

CATHEDRAL

CHAPEL

MOSQUE

End

THYME

TARRAGON

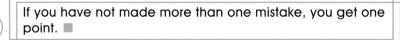

If you have not made more than one mistake, you get one point. ■

HURRAY FOR CHANGE

Link the following numbers and words by numerical order (from small to big) and alphabetical order, respectively. You cannot change your mind once you have traced a line nor link two elements twice. Start with the number marked "Begin" and end with the word marked "End."

Example: bear; algae; dog; lichen; mouse; fungi

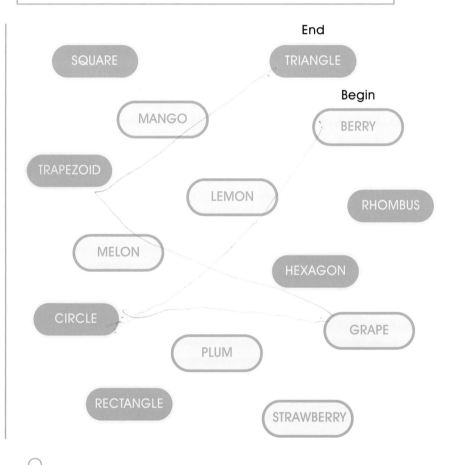

End

SQUARE   TRIANGLE

Begin

MANGO   BERRY

TRAPEZOID

LEMON

RHOMBUS

MELON

HEXAGON

CIRCLE   GRAPE

PLUM

RECTANGLE   STRAWBERRY

If you have not made more than one mistake, you get one point. ■

THE RIGHT WORD

Find the word that corresponds to the definition.

1 - mineralized or otherwise preserved remains or traces (such as foot-prints) of animals, plants, and other organisms

fossils

2 - ring with a flat bottom fixed on a leather strap, usually hung from each side of a saddle to create a footrest for the rider on a riding animal

stirrups

3 - smooth, round object produced by certain mollusks, primarily oysters

pearl

4 - digit of the foot of a human or animal

toe

5 - shelter consisting of sheets of fabric or other material draped over or attached to a frame of poles

tent

If you have not made more than one mistake, you get one point. ▤

THE RIGHT WORD

Find the word that corresponds to the definition.

1 - hair that grows on a man's chin, cheeks, neck, and the area above the upper lip

whiskers

2 - tracked armored fighting vehicle, designed primarily to engage enemy forces by the use of direct fire

tank

3 - distinctive mark or impression made upon an object, most often paper

seal

4 - religion and philosophy from ancient India based on the teachings of the Buddha

Hindu *Hin Buddhism*

5 - form of expression in which an implicit meaning is concealed or contradicted by the explicit meaning of the expression

If you have not made more than one mistake, you get one point. ■

ENTANGLED FIGURES

Examine the figure below; then determine which three of the nine figures below it are combined to form the figure.

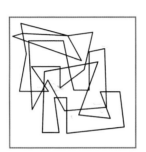

117

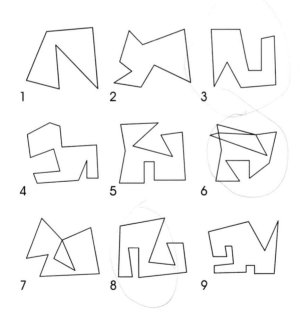

1

2

3

4

5

6

7

8

9

If you have found at least two of the three figures, you get one point. ■

ENTANGLED FIGURES

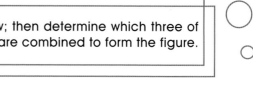

Examine the figure below; then determine which three of the nine figures below it are combined to form the figure.

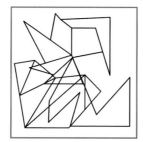

118

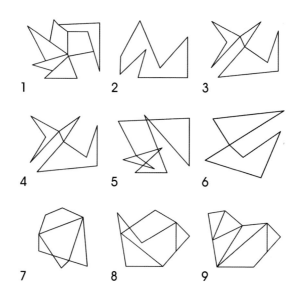

1   2   3

4   5   6

7   8   9

If you have found at least two of the three figures, you get one point. ▥

ELEPHANT'S MEMORY

Memorize the twenty-five words in the grid below. Then turn the page to continue. It is easier if you group the words by category.

rubythroat	gun	crocus	chair	bronze
violet	aluminum	stool	sparrow	missile
bomb	table	blackbird	bed	narcissus
copper	carbine	iron	tulip	canary
chickadee	begonia	dresser	bow	silver

ELEPHANT'S MEMORY (continued)

> Find the twenty-five words you memorized from the pre-
> vious page among the seventy words in the grid below.

capricorn	aluminum	rain	narcissus	Monday
crocus	rock	novel	liqueur	cap
wine	desert	chickadee	intelligence	bow
stone	Saturday	hat	chair	plain
canary	rest	haze	virgo	tulip
book	silver	rubythroat	gallop	stetson
carbine	tragedy	vodka	bronze	Wednesday
hint	stool	begonia	hill	sparrow
aries	valley	snow	comedy	beret
iron	blackbird	cobble	gun	poetry
fineness	rum	bed	Sunday	table
bomb	frost	tundra	libra	violet
leo	Thursday	missile	sand	fog
trick	copper	biographer	dresser	champagne

Please check the answers against the previous page.

> If you have found at least fifteen of the twenty-five words, you
> get one point.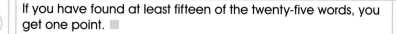

ELEPHANT'S MEMORY

Memorize the twenty-five words in the grid below. Then turn the page to continue. It is easier if you group the words by category.

hammer	trout	cold	orange	plane
cherry	angina	screwdriver	school	otitis
university	salmon	high school	file	tuna
saw	measles	almond	college	apple
peach	institute	flounder	varicella	cod

ELEPHANT'S MEMORY (continued)

Find the twenty-five words you memorized from the previous page among the seventy words in the grid below.

institute	war	file	letter	cod
leg	verb	roast beef	planet	wheel
apple	star	acrobat	orange	veal
dozen	angina	calf	name	high school
brake	trapeze	flounder	saw	skirt
plane	murder	comet	adverb	measles
phrase	million	school	ribs	hundred
clown	almond	light	trout	assassination
T-bone	arm	pronoun	galaxy	hammer
screwdriver	meteorite	tuna	word	juggler
billion	cold	theft	paragraph	otitis
university	wheel	adjective	cherry	finger
breeder	fishing	peach	horn	college
salmon	text	outrage	varicella	scallop

Please check the answers against the previous page.

If you have found at least fifteen of the twenty-five words, you get one point.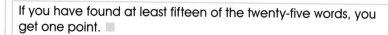

WHERE IS THE ODD ONE?

Find the odd one hidden in each series.

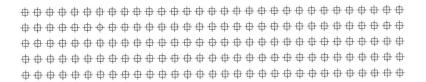

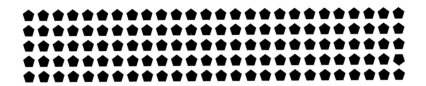

123

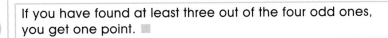

If you have found at least three out of the four odd ones, you get one point.

WHERE IS THE ODD ONE?

Find the odd one hidden in each series.

```
IIIIIIIIIIIIIIIIIIIIIIIIIIIIIIIIIIIIIIIIIIIIIII
IIIIIIIIIIIIIIIIIIIIIIIIIIIIIIIIIIIIIIIIIIIIIII
IIIIIIIIIIIIIIIIIIIIIIIIIIIIIIIIIIIIIIIIIIIIIIIII
IIIIIIIIIIIIIIIIIIIIIIIIIIIIIIIIIIIIIIIIIIIIIIIII
IIIIIIIIIIIIIIIIIIIIIIIIIIIIIIIIIIIIIIIIIIIIIII
```

```
SSSSSSSSeSSSSSSSSSSSSSSSSSSSSSSSSSSSSSSSSSSSSSSSSSSSSSS
SSSSSSSSSSSSSSSSSSSSSSSSSSSSSSSSSSSSSSSSSSSSSSSSSSSSSSS
SSSSSSSSSSSSSSSSSSSSSSSSSSSSSSSSSSSSSSSSSSSSSSSSSSSSSSS
SSSSSSSSSSSSSSSSSSSSSSSSSSSSSSSSSSSSSSSSSSSSSSSSSSSSSSS
```

```
HHHHHHHHHHHHHHHHHHHHHHHHHHHHHHHHHHHHHHHHHHHHHHHHH
HHHHHHHHHHHHHHHHHHHHHHHHHHHHHHHHHHHHHHHHHHHHHHHHH
HHHHHHHHHHHHHHHHHHHHHHHHHHHHHHHHHHHHHHHHHHHHHHHHИ
HHHHHHHHHHHHHHHHHHHHHHHHHHHHHHHHHHHHHHHHHHHHHHHHH
```

If you have found at least three out of the four odd ones, you get one point.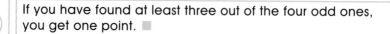

SPELLING MISTAKES

Find the correct spelling of each word among three different options.

hypoglicemia	hippoglycemia	hypoglycemia
circumstence	cyrcumstance	circumstance
enciclopedia	encyclopedia	encycloppedia
multilingual	multylingual	multilyngual
mathemmatics	mathematics	mathemattics
southestern	southeeastern	southeastern
asthma	athsma	ashma
playwright	playright	playwrite
psychotherapist	psichotherapist	psychotherrapist
ballistic	ballystic	balistic
conservattionist	conservationnist	conservationist
neuroscientist	neuroscyentist	neurroscientist
evollution	evvolution	evolution

125

If you have found at least eight correct answers, you get one point. ▀

SPELLING MISTAKES

Find the correct spelling of each word among three different options.

session	sesson	sesion
breaststrok	breastroke	breaststroke
searchablle	sercheable	searchable
geographiccally	geographically	geographicaly
domminance	dominnance	dominance
reluctansy	relluctancy	reluctancy
amunition	amunnition	ammunition
contingent	continjent	continngent
invulnnerable	invulerable	invulnerrable
sugestion	suggesstion	suggestion
incongruously	incongrously	inkongruously
government	governement	goverment
depyction	deppiction	depiction
aftermmath	aftemath	aftermath

126

If you have found at least eight correct answers, you get one point. ▦

WRITING IN THE STARS

Complete the two stars using six of the nine words in the box. Arrows indicate the direction of each word.

TYPHOON
STATION
FREEZER
TRILOGY
SOLVENT
STEEPLE
EPISODE
SULFATE
PORTION

127

HARDTOP
HOSPICE
BRIGADE
BREADTH
BIBELOT
MODESTY
GRAVITY
MEETING
DISGUST

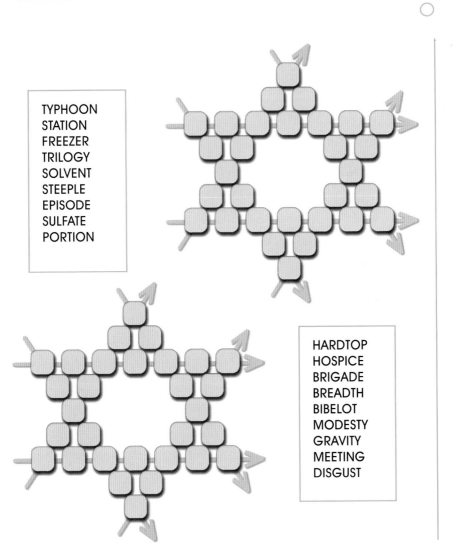

If you correctly filled at least one star, you get one point. ■

WRITING IN THE STARS

Complete the two stars using six of the nine words in the box. Arrows indicate the direction of each word.

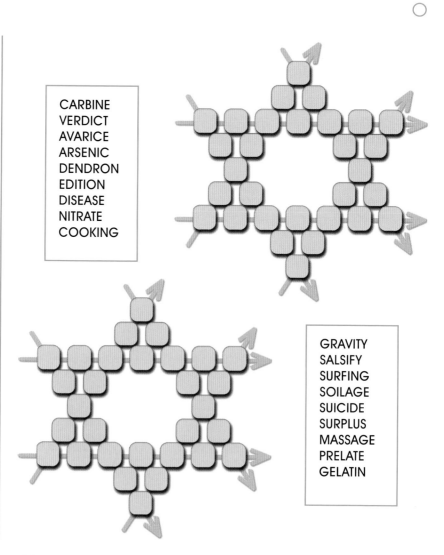

CARBINE
VERDICT
AVARICE
ARSENIC
DENDRON
EDITION
DISEASE
NITRATE
COOKING

128

GRAVITY
SALSIFY
SURFING
SOILAGE
SUICIDE
SURPLUS
MASSAGE
PRELATE
GELATIN

If you correctly filled at least one star, you get one point. ■

OBJECTS, WHERE ARE YOU?

Take a careful look at the shape and location of the six items in this grid. Then turn the page to continue.

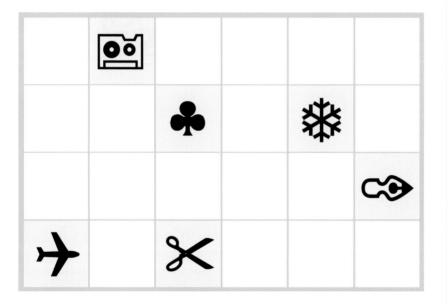

OBJECTS, WHERE ARE YOU? (continued)

Place each of the six pictures from the preceding page in the correct rectangles below.

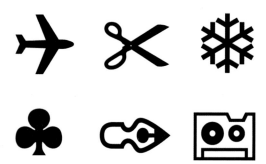

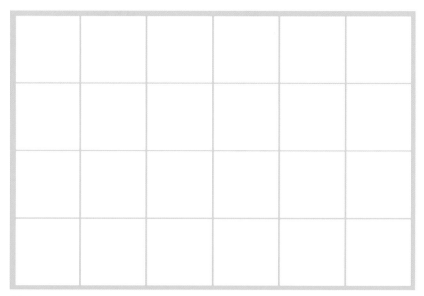

Please check your answers against the previous page.

If you have not made more than two mistakes, you get one point. ■

OBJECTS, WHERE ARE YOU?

Take a careful look at the shape and location of the six items in this grid. Then turn the page to continue.

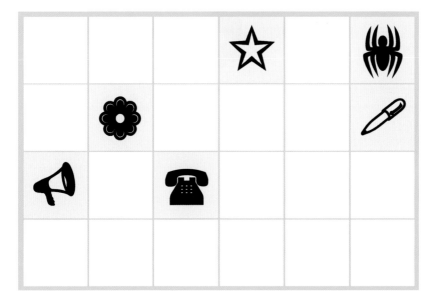

OBJECTS, WHERE ARE YOU? (continued)

Place each of the six pictures from the preceding page in the correct rectangles below.

132

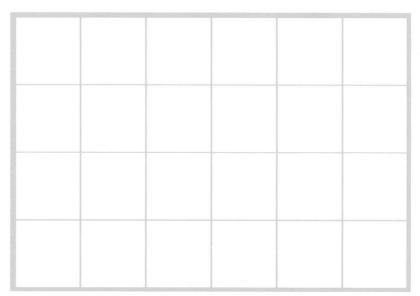

Please check your answers against the previous page.

If you have not made more than two mistakes, you get one point. ■

MOSAICS

Take a careful look at the six elements below and try to determine which ones are not part of the figure below. Beware, some pictures might just have been turned around!

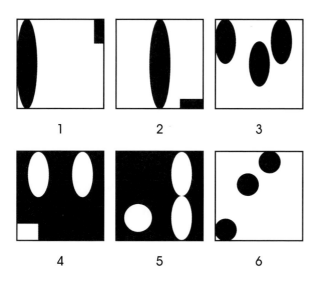

1

2

3

4

5

6

133

If you have not made more than one mistake, you get one point. ▪

MOSAICS

Take a careful look at the six elements below and try to determine which ones are not part of the figure below. Beware, some pictures might just have been turned around!

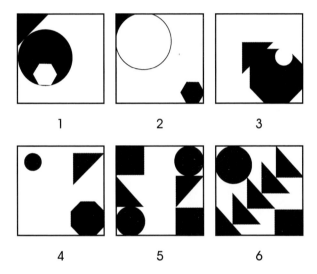

1   2   3

4   5   6

134

If you have not made more than one mistake, you get one point. ▬

ANAGRAMS

The letters of the ten following words have been mixed up. They are all related to Medicine. The first letter of each word is given as a clue.

ETBLAT: T _ablet_

BESETAID: D _iabetes_

UEROIECSIENN: N _euroscience_

EAHTLHACRE: H _ealthcare_

INATOIVCCAN: V _accination_

PTMOYSM: S _ysmptom_

NEMIOTNT: O _intment_

RTORYABLAO: L _aboratory_

ENTSITRDY: D _____

IIEFWMD: M _idwife_

135

If you have found at least six words, you get one point. ▥

ANAGRAMS

The letters of the ten following words have been mixed up. They are all related to Architecture. The first letter of each word is given as a clue.

GIINUBLD: B_____

IEOCRNC: C_____

MMDRISEON: M_____

LOCMNU: C_____

AABSIILC: B_____

ESBTRUST: B_____

SKYTOENE: K_____

NNOOACDLE: C_____

YRPMIDA: P_____

SSCARPEYKR: S_____

If you have found at least six words, you get one point. ▪

BASKETBALL IN NEW YORK

Determine the minimal number of moves needed to move from the configuration in Figure A to the configuration of Figure B. Follow these rules:
- balls may only move out of baskets upwards
- you may not place more than three balls in one basket
- you may only move one ball at a time

A

B

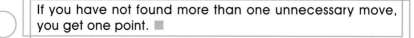

If you have not found more than one unnecessary move, you get one point. ■

BASKETBALL IN NEW YORK

Determine the minimal number of moves needed to move from the configuration in Figure A to the configuration of Figure B. Follow these rules:
- balls may only move out of baskets upwards
- you may not place more than three balls in one basket
- you may only move one ball at a time

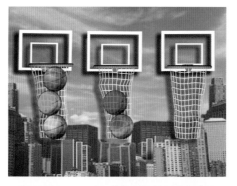

A

B

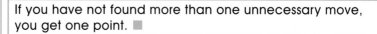

If you have not found more than one unnecessary move, you get one point. ■

WHAT IS THE RECIPE?

Memorize the list of ingredients from the recipe below. You should memorize both the ingredients and their quantity. Then read the recipe carefully (you do not have to memorize it, but it might be useful!). Then turn the page.

LEMON RISOTTO

Ingredients

- 2 cups (500 ml.) rice
- 6 to 8 cups (1500–2000 ml.) chicken stock
- 1 cup (250 ml.) white wine
- zest of 3 lemons
- juice of 1 lemon
- 1 white onion, finely chopped
- pinch of saffron threads
- 4 tbls (60 ml.) oil
- 1 cup (500 ml.) shaved Parmesan cheese
- 1 bunch chives cut into 4–6 cm. sticks

Preparation

Bring the chicken stock to a boil. Heat the oil in a heavy sauce pan, add the onions, lemon zest, and the saffron, cook for 2 minutes, then add the rice and cook for another 2–3 minutes, stirring constantly until the grains become translucent. Stir in the white wine and lemon juice and continue to cook until the wine is absorbed. Add the hot chicken stock one cup (250 ml.) at a time, stirring constantly until the stock is absorbed. Once the rice is tender but still al dente, take away from the heat and add half the amount of Parmesan cheese.

WHAT IS THE RECIPE? (continued)

Find all the ingredients for the recipe on the previous page from among the thirty ingredients below. Strike through the ingredients that were not part of the recipe. Where applicable, write the quantity beside the ingredient.

white onion _____

cauliflower _____

potato _____

zucchini _____

pepper _____

carrots _____

red wine _____

saffron _____

oil _____

butte _____

lemon zest _____

milk _____

coriander _____

eggs _____

rice _____

mozzarella cheese _____

brie _____

bread _____

chicken stock _____

chives _____

flour _____

vinegar _____

white wine _____

lemon juice _____

olives _____

saffron _____

Parmesan cheese _____

garlic _____

tarragon _____

sage _____

Please check your answers against the previous page.

If you have not made more than five mistakes, you get one point.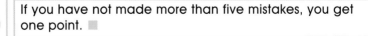

WHAT IS THE RECIPE?

Memorize the list of ingredients from the recipe below. You should memorize both the ingredients and their quantity. Then read the recipe carefully (you do not have to memorize it, but it might be useful!). Then turn the page.

RASPBERRY TRIFLE

Ingredients

- 1/2 cup (125 ml.) sugar
- 1/3 cup (80 ml.) cornstarch
- 3 cups (750 ml.) skim milk
- 2 egg yolks
- 1 teaspoon (5 ml.) vanilla extract
- 1 frozen pound cake (10 3/4 oz.) (300 g.), thawed
- 1 quart (900 g.) raspberries, sliced
- 1 container (8 oz.) (227.5 g.) fat free frozen whipped topping, thawed

Preparation

In a saucepan, stir together the sugar and cornstarch. Gradually add the milk, stirring until smooth. Stir in the beaten egg yolks. Cook over medium heat, stirring constantly, until the mixture comes to a boil. Boil for 2 minutes and remove from the heat. Stir in the vanilla. Refrigerate until chilled. Cut pound cake into 1-inch slices. Arrange half of the slices on bottom of trifle bowl or deep glass bowl. Layer with half the berries, half the custard, and half the whipped topping. Repeat the layers with the remaining ingredients beginning with the pound cake and ending with the whipped topping.

WHAT IS THE RECIPE? (continued)

Find all the ingredients for the recipe on the previous page from among the thirty ingredients below. Strike through the ingredients that were not part of the recipe. Where applicable, write the quantity beside the ingredient.

apples _____
pears _____
strawberries _____
plums _____
grapefruit _____
chocolate chips _____
coffee _____
caramel _____
whipped topping _____
corn syrup _____
vanilla extract _____
yogurt _____
butter _____
sugar _____
raspberries _____
cornstarch _____
egg whites _____
flour _____
skim milk _____
rum _____
pound cake _____
marshmallows _____
walnuts _____
toasted almonds _____
brown sugar _____
soya milk _____
egg yolk _____
honey _____
baking powder _____
rhubarb _____

Please check your answers against the previous page.

If you have not made more than five mistakes, you get one point.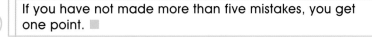

WHAT IS THE DIFFERENCE?

Identify the nine differences between these two pictures.

143

If you have found out at least seven differences, you get one point. ▦

WHAT IS THE DIFFERENCE?

Identify the nine differences between these two pictures.

If you have found out at least seven differences, you get one point.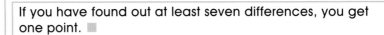

POINTS OF VIEW

Take a careful look at the location of the seven objects in this landscape.

145

The image below shows the same landscape as seen from above. Determine as fast as possible where you would stand in the scenery to view the landscape as it appears in the top image.

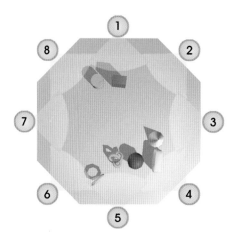

If you have found the correct answer, you get one point. ▦

POINTS OF VIEW

Take a careful look at the location of the seven objects in this landscape.

146

The image below shows the same landscape as seen from above. Determine as fast as possible where you would stand in the scenery to view the landscape as it appears in the top image.

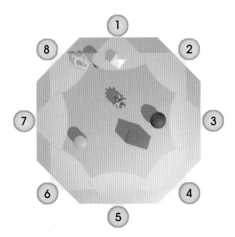

If you have found the correct answer, you get one point. ■

THE MYSTERY WORD

Find the seven-letter word hidden in each grid. The letters may follow each other horizontally or vertically but not diagonally.

A	R	P	R
N	C	H	I
G	Y	L	V
O	N	E	E

P	T	I	L
E	R	N	E
S	O	I	G
S	B	A	R

C	S	P	H
O	A	N	Y
M	P	E	I
A	L	R	E

G	M	U	E
P	R	A	F
E	G	H	Y
H	I	W	A

If you have found at least three words, you get one point.

THE MYSTERY WORD

Find the eight-letter word hidden in each grid. The letters may follow each other horizontally or vertically but not diagonally.

148

N	E	L	P
I	N	A	A
B	E	L	E
U	A	P	S

S	I	R	O
A	U	O	M
G	N	T	P
N	I	A	U

E	F	E	C
T	O	C	U
R	E	O	L
A	C	N	E

C	O	O	T
C	O	R	C
U	L	L	E
A	I	D	T

If you have found at least three words, you get one point. ▮

SHAPES AND COLORS

Memorize the six figures below. Then turn the page.

SHAPES AND COLORS (continued)

Now try to find the six figures you memorized from the twenty-four figures displayed below.

150

Please check your answers against the previous page.

If you have found at least four figures, you get one point. ■

SHAPES AND COLORS

Memorize the six figures below. Then turn the page.

SHAPES AND COLORS (continued)

Now try to find the six figures you memorized from the twenty-four figures displayed below.

152

Please check your answers against the previous page.

If you have found at least four figures, you get one point. ▪

DECIPHER

> Try to decipher this quotation. Letters are always replaced by the same symbol.

Replace the picture below with a well-known quotation.

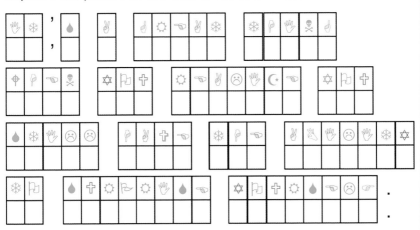

Replace the picture below with a well-known quotation.

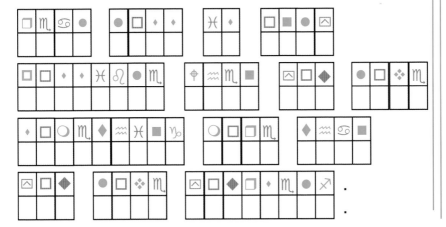

> If you have made fewer than three mistakes, you get one point. ■

DECIPHER

Replace the picture below with a well-known quotation.

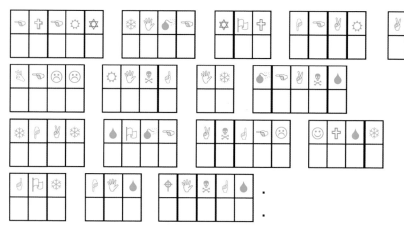

Replace the picture below with a well-known quotation.

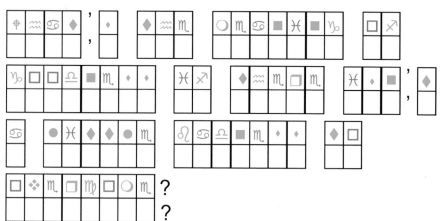

154

PLAY ON WORDS

Find the antonym (opposite) of each word. The first letter is given as a hint.

affirmative: n_____   shy: b_____
forward: b_____   seeks: a_____
below: a_____   remember: f_____
night: d_____   tame: w_____
agnostic: r_____   infantile: m_____

Find which word cannot be a synonym of the four others in each row.

| clueless | restless | fidgety | fretful | twitchy |

| highlight | sunlight | bring out | spotlight | play up |

| godlike | divine | providential | elysian | divinity |

| calm | sharpen | pacify | assuage | appease |

 If you have not made more than five mistakes, you get one point. ▮

PLAY ON WORDS

Find the antonym (opposite) of each word. The first letter is given as a hint.

prevent: p_____   peace: w_____
wise: f_____   harmony: d_____
handy: i_____   despair: h_____
homozygous: h_____ smooth: r_____
break: r_____   malodorous: f_____

Find which word cannot be a synonym of the four others in each row.

| mobile | wondering | nomadic | transient | wandering |

| common | fabulous | terrific | extraordinary | amazing |

| dream | illusion | fantasy | fancy | true |

| completed | deleted | over | terminated | ended |

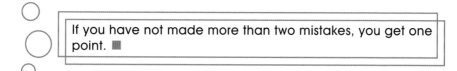

If you have not made more than two mistakes, you get one point. ▦

156

WHO AM I?

Whose life is described below?

I was born on September 11, 1885, in Eastwood, England. My father was a coal miner who drank heavily and my mother was a school-teacher. My childhood was dominated by poverty and friction between my parents. I attended Nottingham High School on a scholarship and later worked as a student teacher for four years. At the age of 22, I matriculated from Nottingham University and pursued a brief teaching career.

My poetry was first published in 1909 by Ford Madox Ford in the *English Review*. The publication of my first novel, *The White Peacock* (1911), launched my writing career. In 1912 I met and fell in love with Frieda von Richthofen. Though she was married with three children, she left her family and we eloped to Bavaria. In 1913 I published one of my most famous literary works, a novel based on my childhood in England. In 1914 Frieda von Richthofen and I married. During World War I, we could not get passports and were constantly harassed by the authorities. In 1917 we were accused of spying for the Germans and expelled from Cornwall.

My best-known work, published privately in Florence in 1928, tells of the love affair between a wealthy, married woman and a man employed on her husband's estate. The book was banned for a period of time in both the United States and United Kingdom for being pornographic. I died in Vence, France, on March 2, 1930.

I am _____

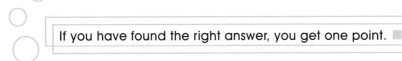

If you have found the right answer, you get one point.

WHO AM I?

Whose life is described below?

I was born in Kumasi, Ghana, on April 8, 1938. I studied at the University of Science and Technology in Kumasi and completed my undergraduate work in economics at Macalester College in St. Paul, Minnesota, in 1961. From 1961 to 1962 I undertook graduate studies in economics in Geneva. I received a Master of Science degree in management as a 1971–1972 Sloan Fellow at the Massachusetts Institute of Technology.

In 1962 I joined the United Nations as an administrative and budget officer with the World Health Organization (WHO) in Geneva, the first of many UN positions that would eventually culminate in my appointment as Secretary General.

I am _____

If you have found the right answer, you get one point.

SLEIGHT OF HAND

Among the six hands below, find the right hands and the left hands. Beware, some of the hands are viewed in a mirror.

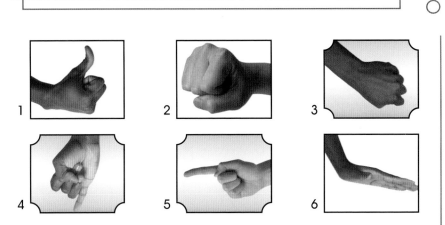

159

Among the six hands below, find the right hands and the left hands. Beware, some of the hands are viewed in a mirror.

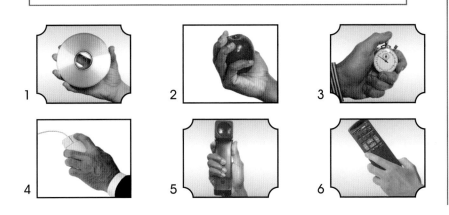

If you have not made more than two mistakes, you get one point. ▪.

SLEIGHT OF HAND

Among the six hands below, find the right hands and the left hands. Beware, some of the hands are viewed in a mirror.

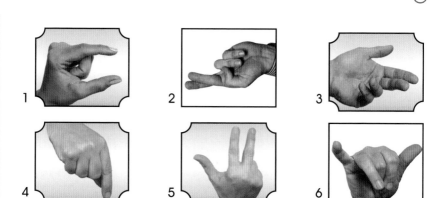

1
2
3
4
5
6

Among the six hands below, find the right hands and the left hands. Beware, some of the hands are viewed in a mirror.

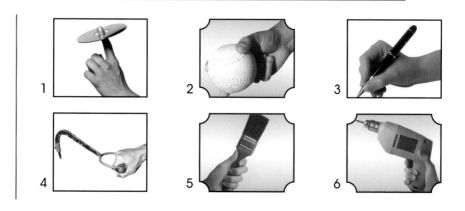

1
2
3
4
5
6

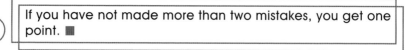

If you have not made more than two mistakes, you get one point. ▥

NO PROBLEM!

> Try to solve these two mathematical problems in your head. If you need to, you can write down the operations on a sheet of paper.

Problem #1

Every hour the kitchen clock gets five minutes faster. The living room clock gets five minutes slower every hour. They were both set at the same time. The kitchen clock displays 3:30 p.m. and the living-room clock displays 12 p.m. What time is it?

_____

Problem #2

Four friends have to go to the other side of the lake. They only have one boat, and this boat is only big enough for two rowers.
Pete can cross one-way in four minutes.
It takes Mark twice as long.
It takes Ivan twice as long as Mark.
It take Juliana twice as long as Ivan.
Pete says they can do it in one hour.

When there are two rowers, the speed is that of the slowest. Is Pete correct? Explain your answer.

_____

> If you have solved at least one problem, you get one point. ■

NO PROBLEM!

Try to solve these two mathematical problems in your head. If you need to, you can write down the operations on a sheet of paper.

Problem #1

Eight bags are filled to 6/7 of their capacity with corn.
Two-thirds are sold to a carrier.
The carrier thinks he then needs six bags to put his corn in.
Can the seller fill up the last two bags with his remaining corn?

Problem #2

At the dry cleaner, wire hangers are put at regular intervals on a round cable. Wire hangers are numbered, starting with one.
When wire hanger 8 is opposite wire hanger 15, then wire hanger 81 is opposite wire hanger 92.
How many wire hangers are there on the cable?

If you have solved at least one problem, you get one point. ■

FIND YOUR WAY

Take a careful look at the figure below, paying special attention to the directional arrows that connect the seven colored circles. Try to memorize the order in which the arrows progress from beginning to end. Then turn the page.

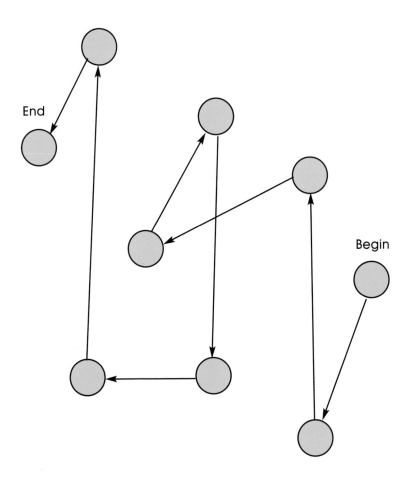

End

Begin

163

FIND YOUR WAY (continued)

Reconstruct the figure from the previous page by drawing the connecting arrows.

164

Please check your answer against the previous page.

If you have not made more than two mistakes, you get one point. ■

FIND YOUR WAY

Take a careful look at the figure below, paying special attention to the directional arrows that connect the seven colored circles. Try to memorize the order in which the arrows progress from beginning to end. Then turn the page.

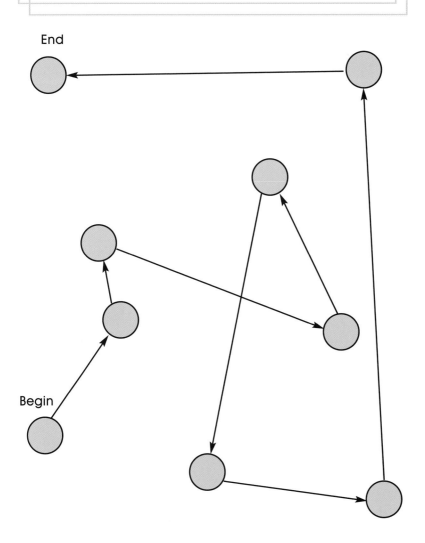

End

Begin

165

FIND YOUR WAY (continued)

Reconstruct the figure from the previous page by drawing the connecting arrows.

Please check your answer against the previous page.

If you have not made more than two mistakes, you get one point. ■

Comments
on scores for level #2

COMMENTS level #2

CALCULATE YOUR RESULTS

Write down in this table the number of points obtained at level #2:

Number of ▦	Number of ▦	Number of ▦	Number of ▦	Number of ▦	TOTAL

COMMENTS ON YOUR SCORE

If you earned 0 to 21 points:

Maybe you didn't score as high as you wanted to here. Don't be discouraged—remember that mental training is a marathon not a sprint! Keep at it!

If you earned 22 to 43 points:

Good work! You have quite a fit and healthy brain. Detailed comments from each cognitive area will help you identify your mental strengths and weaknesses, so you can continue to improve. Keep up the good work!

If you earned 44 to 64 points:

Congratulations! These are great results! You have reached the highest level of these challenging exercises. Keep on training regularly and challenging your brain, and your neurons will be fit for a long long time!

COMMENTS level #2

COMMENTS BY COGNITIVE AREA

Memory score ▇

If you earned 0 to 6 points:
These exercises are meant to be challenging, and it takes time to get in shape. You probably know what you should do to improve: train your neurons!

If you earned 7 to 13 points:
You've got a pretty good memory across the board: verbal, visual semantic, and short-term. Your learning strategy is certainly working for you, and with a bit more training your results will improve even more.

If you earned 14 to 20 points:
Well, seeing your results, it can be said that you have an elephant's memory! You know how to keep up your attention during the learning process, you certainly have a method or mnemonic means to help, and you are used to training your memory. Great work—keep it up!

Language score ▇▇

If you earned 0 to 4 points:
The only way to master the English language is to plunge in. Don't be discouraged—shake your neurons and you will see that language games are not as boring as you think!

If you earned 5 to 9 points:
You are quite familiar with the English language, you know spelling and grammar rules, and your vocabulary is nothing to be ashamed of. The more you challenge yourself linguistically, the better your language skills will be!

If you earned 10 to 14 points:
Seeing your great results, you must be an absolute fan of crosswords and other word games. English has no secrets for you, and you can easily juggle with a very important stock of vocabulary that you probably keep up and enrich thanks to reading and linguistic challenges. Keep it up!

COMMENTS level #2

Attention and concentration score ▥

If you earned 0 to 2 points:

You probably prefer quick-on-your-feet, fast-paced challenges to these attention exercises! Don't be afraid to slow down and focus—a strong attention span is a great asset to have. All you have to do is keep challenging yourself!

If you earned 3 to 5 points:

Way to go! You've got a healthy attention span, and your score in this area reflects that. It's not always easy to focus for long periods of time, and you've certainly proven yourself here! With a bit more practice, your concentration is sure to improve even more!

If you earned 6 to 8 points:

Fabulous work! You've got quite an impressive attention span, and you've earned an excellent score in this area! Your ability to resist distractions and concentrate for long periods of time is a valuable skill to have. Keep your brain active and take care of it!

Logical reasoning score ▪

If you earned 0 to 3 points:

Logic may not be your forte, but don't despair—these exercises were designed to be extremely tricky. Try taking your time when facing logical challenges and organizing the problem with a method or strategy. All you need are some good logical workouts to get your brain in top shape!

If you earned 4 to 8 points:

Good work! It may not come naturally to you, but you have accomplished logic and reasoning skills. You know how to develop and apply methodologies, divide a problem into sub-problems, and recognize various constraints. With a little more training, you'll be a logic pro!

COMMENTS level #2 ─────────

If you earned 9 to 12 points:

You must love mathematical tricks, logic games, and puzzles. Not only is your sense of logic highly developed, but your methodology is also quite impressive, and thanks to your raising of hypotheses and drawing deductions, you always reach your goal! Congratulations. You're a logic superstar!

Visual and spatial score ▮

If you earned 0 to 3 points:

It's not always easy to be able to understand a map or judge at first sight whether a parking spot is big enough for your car. Good work on these challenging exercises—and don't get discouraged. The more you train, the stronger your visual and spatial skills will be!

If you earned 4 to 6 points:

Great work! You are able to situate yourself in space and have a 3-dimensional representation of your environment. Your visual and spatial capacities will only improve with more training. Try picking up some jigsaw puzzles for a start. In no time, you'll be a visual and spatial whiz!

If you earned 7 to 10 points:

With a map, you could go anywhere! You know perfectly how to analyze visual details, evaluate their size and their location, how they are placed in relation to others, and even turn them mentally. In short, your visual and spatial capacities are excellent. Congrats on a job well done!

SOLUTIONS

SOLUTIONS level#1

RIGHT or WRONG? p. 3

1 - Wrong; 2 - Right; 3 - Wrong; 4 - Right; 5 - Right; 6 - Right; 7 - Wrong; 8 - Wrong; 9 - Right; 10 - Wrong; 11 - Right; 12 - Right; 13 - Right; 14 - Wrong; 15 - Right; 16 - Wrong; 17 - Wrong; 18 - Wrong; 19 - Right; 20 - Right

RIGHT or WRONG? p. 4

1 - Right; 2 - Right; 3 - Wrong; 4 - Wrong; 5 - Right; 6 - Wrong; 7 - Wrong; 8 - Right; 9 - Wrong; 10 - Wrong; 11 - Right; 12 - Wrong; 13 - Right; 14 - Right; 15 - Wrong; 16 - Right; 17 - Right; 18 - Wrong; 19 - Wrong; 20 - Wrong

SINGULAR OR PLURAL? p. 5

Singular	Plural
box	children
cheese	feet
criterion	foxes
hemisphere	geese
nail	glasses
shoe	sketches
sock	stairs
tribe	women

SINGULAR OR PLURAL? p. 6

Singular	Plural
bear	halves
city	mice
crane	people
excess	prices
eyelash	sins
mouse	supplies
silver	teeth
speed	thieves

SOLUTIONS level#1 ⸻

TOWERS OF HANOI p. 7

At least four moves are needed to move from A to B:
- yellow ring on stem 2
- purple ring on stem 3
- green ring on stem 2
- purple ring on stem 2

TOWERS OF HANOI p. 8

At least six moves are needed to move from A to B:
- green ring on stem 2
- purple ring on stem 2
- yellow ring on stem 3
- purple ring on stem 1
- green ring on stem 3
- purple ring on stem 3

CHIVALRY p. 9–10

The shield was made of:
- shape #2
- colors #2
- pattern #1

CHIVALRY p. 11–12

The shield was made of:
- shape #3
- colors #1
- pattern #2

THE ODD ONE OUT p. 17

The odd one is the Rockefeller Center, the only American monuments among four British ones.

The odd one is the scalpel, the only surgeon's tool among four gardener's tools.

SOLUTIONS level#1

The odd one is the snail, the only mollusk among four crustaceans.

The odd one is *The Wall*, the only Pink Floyd song among four songs by Marilyn Monroe.

The odd one is Michael Shumacher, the only F1 pilot among four basketball players.

THE ODD ONE OUT p. 18

The odd one is the Sun, the only star among four planets.

The odd one is Tom Cruise, the only actor among four writers.

The odd one is Morocco, the only African country among four European country.

The odd one is cod, the only fish among four meats.

The odd one is fir, the only softwood tree among four harwood ones.

TURNING AROUND p. 19

The two figures are mirror images.

TURNING AROUND p. 20

The two figures are identical.

THIS STORY IS FULL OF BLANKS p. 21

Some said he had been a Russian spy, others that he was related to one of Europe's royal families. Nearly all his acquaintances took advantage of his incredible hospitality. In his castle, he gave the most fabulous parties one could remember, and the most amazing thing of all is that guests were never quite sure who the host was. He had also lived in the jungle for years, and ornaments in his home paid tribute to the animal world he had encountered there. You could not imagine what amazing thing this man was going to accomplish next.

THIS STORY IS FULL OF BLANKS p. 22

Oxford professor James Blew was quietly sitting in his study when an urgent late night phone call abruptly interrupted him from his reading. The elderly Headmaster of the university had disappeared for more than two days now, and the police phone call did not bring good news. They had found his body in a car near the Scotland castle where he usually liked to go during his weekends during the summer season. The police investigation would have to start soon.

MOVING CHARACTERS p. 23

The replaced characters are in red.

MOVING CHARACTERS p. 24

The replaced characters are in red.

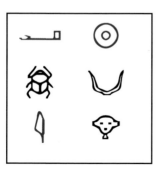

SOLUTIONS level#1 ——————————

TIDY IT UP! p. 25

Martial arts	Team sports	Winter sports	Water sports
aïkido	basketball	bobsled	waterskiing
judo	soccer	ice hockey	surfing
karate	handball	luge	sailing
Thai boxing	rugby	skiing	windsurfing
tae kwon do	volleyball	snowboarding	wakeboarding

TIDY IT UP! p. 26

Literary authors	Modern bands	Classical composers	Painters
Henry James	The Rolling Stones	Mozart	Leonardo Da Vinci
Nathaniel Hawthorne	Pink Floyd	Debussy	Salvador Dali
F. Scott Fitzgerald	Texas	Berlioz	J. M. Basquiat
John Irving	The Black Eyed Peas	Schubert	Andy Warhol
James Joyce	The Doors	Chopin	Lucian Freud

HURRAY FOR CHANGE p. 27

10 ; MAMBO ; 253 ; RUMBA ; 1000 ; SALSA ; 1010 ; SAMBA ; 9652 ; TANGO; 96538 ; TWIST ; 96856 ; WALTZ

SOLUTIONS level#1 —————

HURRAY FOR CHANGE p. 28

DEGREE ; 236 ; INCH ; 2326 ; METER ; 3256 ; OUNCE ; 23652 ; SECOND ; 23656 ; VOLT ; 32656 ; WATT ; 36256

THE RIGHT WORD p. 29

1 - diameter

2 - pasta

3 - dynasty

4 - pen

5 - silhouette

THE RIGHT WORD p. 30

1 - manga

2 - dam

3 - chess

4 - diabetes

5 - rabbits

ENTANGLED FIGURES p. 31

The three elements are: 2; 6; 9

ENTANGLED FIGURES p. 32

The three elements are: 1; 3; 5

SOLUTIONS level#1

WHERE IS THE ODD ONE? p. 37

The odd one is in red.

θθθθθθθθθθθθθθθθθθθθθθθθθθθθθθθθθθθθθθθθθθθθθθ
θθθθθθθθθθθθθθθθθθθθθθθθθθθθθθθθθθθθθθθθθθθθθθ
θθθθθθθθθθθθθθθθθθθθθθθθθθθθθθθθθθθθθθθθθθθθθθ
θθθθθθθθθθθθθθθθθθθθθθθθθθθθθθθθθθθθθθθθθθθθθθ
θθθθθθθθθθθθθθθθθθθθθθθθθθθθθθθθθθθθθθθθθθθθθθ

◎◎◎◎◎◎◎◎◎◎◎◎◎◎◎◎◎◎◎◎◎◎◎◎◎◎◎◎◎◎◎◎◎◎◎◎◎
◎◎◎◎◎◎◎◎◎◎◎◎◎◎◎◎◎◎◎◎◎◎◎◎◎◎◎◎◎◎◎◎◎◎◎◎◎
◎◎◎◎⊙◎◎◎◎◎◎◎◎◎◎◎◎◎◎◎◎◎◎◎◎◎◎◎◎◎◎◎◎◎◎◎◎
◎◎◎◎◎◎◎◎◎◎◎◎◎◎◎◎◎◎◎◎◎◎◎◎◎◎◎◎◎◎◎◎◎◎◎◎◎
◎◎◎◎◎◎◎◎◎◎◎◎◎◎◎◎◎◎◎◎◎◎◎◎◎◎◎◎◎◎◎◎◎◎◎◎◎

ᘖᘖᘖᘖᘖᘖᘖᘖᘖᘖᘖᘖᘖᘖᘖᘖᘖᘖᘖᘖᘖᘖᘖᘖᘖᘖᘖᘖᘖ
ᘖᘖᘖᘖᘖᘖᘖᘖᘖᘖᘖᘖᘖᘖᘖᘖᘖ♀ᘖᘖᘖᘖᘖᘖᘖᘖᘖᘖᘖ
ᘖᘖᘖᘖᘖᘖᘖᘖᘖᘖᘖᘖᘖᘖᘖᘖᘖᘖᘖᘖᘖᘖᘖᘖᘖᘖᘖᘖᘖ
ᘖᘖᘖᘖᘖᘖᘖᘖᘖᘖᘖᘖᘖᘖᘖᘖᘖᘖᘖᘖᘖᘖᘖᘖᘖᘖᘖᘖᘖ

➝➝➝➝➝➝➝➝➝➝➝➝➝➝➝➝➝➝➝➝➝➝➝➝➝➝➝➝➝➝➝
➝➝➝➝➝➝➝➝➝➝➝➝➝➝➝➝➝➝➝➝➝➝➝➝➝➝➝➝➝➝↩
➝➝➝➝➝➝➝➝➝➝➝➝➝➝➝➝➝➝➝➝➝➝➝➝➝➝➝➝➝➝➝
➝➝➝➝➝➝➝➝➝➝➝➝➝➝➝➝➝➝➝➝➝➝➝➝➝➝➝➝➝➝➝

WHERE IS THE ODD ONE? p. 38

The odd one is in red.

{{{
{{{
{{{
{{}{{
{{{

181

SOLUTIONS level#1 ————————

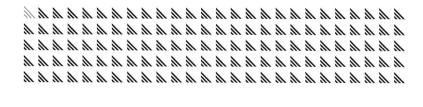

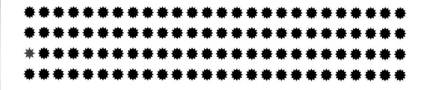

SPELLING MISTAKES p. 39

constitutional; harmony; comedy; millionnaire; obsolete; armament; literally; multiplicity; currently; elephant; sustainability; cowardice; atmosphere; furniture

SPELLING MISTAKES p. 40

strawberry; impressive; loyalty ; expression; parallel; medicine; eligibility; miniature; therapist; philosophy; disagreement; humiliation; powerfully; orchestra

SOLUTIONS level#1

WRITING IN THE STARS p. 41

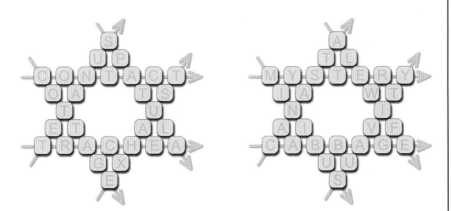

WRITING IN THE STARS p. 42

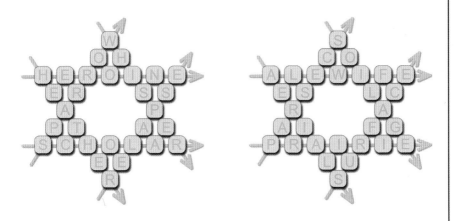

MOSAICS p. 47

Items 1, 2, and 3 do not belong to the figure.

MOSAICS p. 48
Items 1 and 2 do not belong to the figure.

ANAGRAMS p. 49

SHOOTING; CAMERA; ACTRESS; CASTING; ANIMATION; SUBTITLES; DIA-LOGUE; SCENARIO; DIRECTOR; SOUNDTRACK

ANAGRAMS p. 50

FORECAST; TEMPERATURE; FAHRENHEIT; ATMOSPHERE; CLIMATE; SUN-LIGHT; TORNADO; HURRICANE; SATELLITE; BAROMETER

BASKETBALL IN NEW YORK p. 51

You need at least four ball moves to reach B from A:
- purple ball in basket #1
- orange ball in basket #2
- purple ball in basket #3
- blue ball in basket #3

BASKETBALL IN NEW YORK p. 52

You need at least five ball moves to reach B from A:
- purple ball in basket #3
- yellow ball in basket #3
- green ball in basket #3
- orange ball in basket #2
- green ball in basket #1

SOLUTIONS level#1

WHAT IS THE DIFFERENCE? p. 57

WHAT IS THE DIFFERENCE? p. 58

SOLUTIONS level # 1 ———————

POINTS OF VIEW p. 59

You would be at location #2

POINTS OF VIEW p. 60

You would be at location #4

THE MYSTERY WORD p. 61

STYLIST; FURRIER; TOURISM; EYELASH

THE MYSTERY WORD p. 62

SECURITY; PROPERTY; MOISTURE; PRINCESS

DECIPHER p. 67

"People hurt the ones they love. That's how it is all around the world." (*The Green Mile*)

DECIPHER p. 68

"I was out saving the galaxy when your grandfather was still in diapers." (*Star Trek*)

"You can't buy the necessities of life with cookies." (*Edward Scissorhands*)

PLAY ON WORDS p. 69

beautiful - ugly	forbidden - allowed
rich - poor	true - false
close - open	accept - reject
long - short	admirable - despisable
discreet - indiscreet	quiet - loud

problematic is not a synonym of the four other words.
tell is not a synonym of the four other words.
meditate is not a synonym of the four other words.
take off is not a synonym of the four other words.

SOLUTIONS level#1

PLAY ON WORDS p. 70

small - big
raw - cooked
complicate - simplify
busy - idle
easy - hard

careful - careless
increasing - decreasing
empty - full
less - more
few - many

tranquil is not a synonym of the four other words.
rigid is not a synonym of the four other words.
pride is not a synonym of the four other words.
relativity is not a synonym of the four other words.

WHO AM I? p. 71

I am Betty Friedan.

WHO AM I? p. 72

I am Elizabeth Taylor.

SLEIGHT OF HAND p. 73

1: right; 2: right; 3: right; 4: left; 5: left; 6: right
1: left; 2: right; 3: right; 4: right; 5: left; 6: right

SLEIGHT OF HAND p. 74

1: left; 2: right; 3: left; 4: right; 5: left; 6: right
1: right; 2: left; 3: left; 4: right; 5: left; 6: right

SOLUTIONS level#1 ——————

NO PROBLEM! p. 75

Problem #1

Convert all the measurements into feet, then do the following calculations:
25 × 10 = 250
30 × 100 ÷ 12 = 250
7 × 7 = 49

The total length is 549 feet.

Problem #2

On day 39, the algae covers half the pool.
On day 38, the algae covers half this surface, which is one quarter.
Therefore, the algae needs 38 days to cover the quarter of the surface of the pool.

NO PROBLEM! p. 76

Problem #1

5 ÷ 100 × 25,000 = $1,250
The first car dealer offers a discount of $1,250.
4 ÷ 100 × 22,000 = $880
The first car dealer offers a discount of $880.
The biggest discount is the one offered by the first car seller.
25,000 − 1250 = $23,750
With the discount, the first model costs $23,750.
22,000 − 880 = $21,120
With the discount, the second model costs $21,120.
The cheapest vehicle, with or without a discount, remains the second one.

Problem #2

Mister Martin only has four jam jars, one of each flavor!

SOLUTIONS level#2 ————————

RIGHT or WRONG? p. 89

1 - Wrong; 2 - Right; 3 - Right; 4 - Wrong; 5 - Wrong; 6 - Right; 7 - Wrong; 8 - Wrong; 9 - Right; 10 - Right; 11 - Right; 12 - Wrong; 13 - Wrong; 14 - Right; 15 - Right; 16 - Right; 17 - Wrong; 18 - Right; 19 - Right; 20 - Wrong

RIGHT or WRONG? p. 90

1 - Right; 2 - Right; 3 - Wrong; 4 - Right; 5 - Right; 6 - Wrong; 7 - Right; 8 - Wrong; 9 - Wrong; 10 - Right; 11 - Right; 12 - Right; 13 - Wrong; 14 - Right; 15 - Wrong; 16 - Right; 17 - Wrong; 18 - Right; 19 - Right; 20 - Wrong

ADJECTIVE OR NOUN? p. 91

Adjectives	Nouns
big	apple
broken	furniture
clumsy	helium
funny	honor
mad	loneliness
old	man
tired	property
weird	way

ADJECTIVE OR NOUN? p. 92

Adjectives	Nouns
certain	certainty
crazy	charity
horrible	evidence
horrid	folly
pitiless	horror
restless	kindness
terrible	madness
useless	pity

SOLUTIONS level#2

TOWERS OF HANOI p. 93

At least nine moves are needed to move from A to B:
- purple ring on stem 1
- blue ring on stem 2
- purple ring on stem 2
- green ring on stem 3
- purple ring on stem 3
- yellow ring on stem 2
- purple ring on stem 1
- green ring on stem 2
- purple ring on stem 2

TOWERS OF HANOI p. 94

At least seven moves are needed to move from A to B:
- purple ring on stem 1
- green ring on stem 2
- purple ring on stem 2
- yellow ring on stem 1
- purple ring on stem 3
- green ring on stem 1
- purple ring on stem 1

CHIVALRY p. 95–96

The shield was made of:
- shape #4
- colors #2
- pattern #1

CHIVALRY p. 97–98

The shield was made of:
- shape #5
- colors #1
- pattern #2

THE ODD ONE OUT p. 103

The odd one is Montreal, the only Canadian city among four American ones.

The odd one is Faraday, which is not a temperature measure.

The odd one is Journey, the only American band among four British bands.

The odd one is *Raffaello*, the only painter among four explorers.

The odd one is stetson, the only hat among four types of shoes.

THE ODD ONE OUT p. 104

The odd one is eucalyptus, the only tree among four mushrooms.

The odd one is *The Godfather*, the only film not directed by Woody Allen.

The odd one is Franco, the only Spanish leader among four British prime ministers.

The odd one is violin, the only string instrument among four wind instruments.

The odd one is trout, the only freshwater fish among four saltwater.

TURNING AROUND p. 105

Figures 1 and 2 are identical and figure 3 is a mirror image.

TURNING AROUND p. 106

Figures 1 and 2 are identical and figure 3 is a mirror image.

THIS STORY IS FULL OF BLANKS p. 107

During the last year of young David's boyhood, he saw his mother but seldom, and she became for him just a woman with whom he had once lived. Still he could not get her figure out of his mind and as he grew older it became more definite. When he was twelve years old he went to the Bentley farm to live. Old Jesse came into town and fairly demanded that he be given charge of the boy.

THIS STORY IS FULL OF BLANKS p. 108

But the doctor could not of course come to Tomalin with them, though this was never discussed, since just then the conversation was violently interrupted by a sudden terrific detonation, that shook the house and sent birds skimming panic-stricken all over the garden. Target practice in the Sierra Madre. The Consul had been half aware of it in his sleep earlier. Puffs of smoke went drifting high over the rocks below Popo at the end of the valley. Three black vultures came tearing through the trees low over the roof with soft hoarse cries like the cries of love. Driven at unaccustomed speed by their fear they seemed almost to capsize, keeping close together, but balancing at different angles to avoid collision.

MOVING CHARACTERS p. 109

No characters were replaced! All the characters of the second series were identical to the characters in the first series.

MOVING CHARACTERS p. 110

Replaced characters are in red.

TIDY IT UP! p. 111

Seas	Lakes	Oceans	Rivers
Caspian	Victoria	Atlantic	Amur
Red	Ness	Pacific	Amazon
Mediterranean	Baikal	Indian	Thames
Bering	Michigan	Arctic	Nile
China	Great Salt	Southern	Mississippi

TIDY IT UP! p. 112

Weight	Length	Duration	Liquid measure
ton	mile	minute	quart
stone	yard	second	gallon
ounce	feet	hour	pint
pound	inch	millisecond	liter
kilogram	meter	nanosecond	fluid ounce

HURRAY FOR CHANGE p. 113

CATHEDRAL; CHIVE; CHAPEL; CORIANDER; CHURCH; MINT; MONASTERY; PARSLEY; MOSQUE; SAGE; SYNAGOGUE; TARRAGON; TEMPLE; THYME

SOLUTIONS level#2

HURRAY FOR CHANGE p. 114

BERRY; CIRCLE; GRAPE; HEXAGON; LEMON; RECTANGLE; MANGO; RHOMBUS; MELON; SQUARE; PLUM; TRAPEZOID; STRAWBERRY; TRIANGLE

THE RIGHT WORD p. 115

1 - fossil

2 - stirrup

3 - pearl

4 - toe

5 - tent

THE RIGHT WORD p. 116

1 - beard

2 - tank

3 - stamp

4 - Buddhism

5 - irony

ENTANGLED FIGURES p. 117

The three elements are: 3; 6; 8

ENTANGLED FIGURES p. 118

The three elements are: 1; 2; 9

SOLUTIONS level#2

WHERE IS THE ODD ONE? p. 123

The odd one is in red.

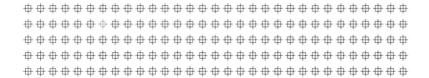

WHERE IS THE ODD ONE? p. 124

The odd one is in red.

SOLUTIONS level #2

```
IIIIIIIIIIIIIIIIIIIIIIIIIIIIIIIIIIIIIIIIIIIIIIIIIII
IIIIIIIIIIIIIIIIIIIIIIIIIIIIIIIIIIIIIIIIIIIIIIIIIII
IIIIIIIIIIIIIIIIIIIIIIIIIIIIIIIIIIIIIIIIIIIIIIIIIII
IIIIIIIIIIIIIIIIIIIIIIIIIIIIIIIIIIIIIIIIIIIIIIIIIII
IIIIIIIIIIIIIIIIIIIIIIIIIIIIIIIIIIIIIIIIIIIIIIIIIII
```

```
§§§§§§§2§§§§§§§§§§§§§§§§§§§§§§§§§§§§§§§§§§§§§§§§§§§§
§§§§§§§§§§§§§§§§§§§§§§§§§§§§§§§§§§§§§§§§§§§§§§§§§§§§§
§§§§§§§§§§§§§§§§§§§§§§§§§§§§§§§§§§§§§§§§§§§§§§§§§§§§§
§§§§§§§§§§§§§§§§§§§§§§§§§§§§§§§§§§§§§§§§§§§§§§§§§§§§§
```

```
HHHHHHHHHHHHHHHHHHHHHHHHHHHHHHHHHHHHHHHHHHHHHHHHH
HHHHHHHHHHHHHHHHHHHHHHHHHHHHHHHHHHHHHHHHHHHHHHHHH
HHHHHHHHHHHHHHHHHHHHHHHHHHHHHHHHHHHHHHHHHHHHHHHHHИ
HHHHHHHHHHHHHHHHHHHHHHHHHHHHHHHHHHHHHHHHHHHHHHHHHH
```

SPELLING MISTAKES p. 125

hypoglycemia; circumstance; encyclopedia; multilingual; mathematics; southeastern; asthma; playwright; psychotherapist; ballistic; conservationist; neuroscientist; evolution; conspiracy

SPELLING MISTAKES p. 126

session; breaststroke; searchable; geographically; dominance; reluctancy; ammunition; contingent; invulnerable; suggestion; incongruously; government; depiction; aftermath

SOLUTIONS level#2

WRITING IN THE STARS p. 127

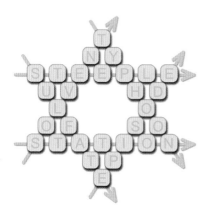

WRITING IN THE STARS p. 128

SOLUTIONS level#2

MOSAICS p. 133

Items 2, 5, and 6 do not belong to the figure.

MOSAICS p. 134

Items 1, 4, and 6 do not belong to the figure.

ANAGRAMS p. 135

TABLET; DIABETES; NEUROSCIENCE; HEALTHCARE; VACCINATION; SYMPTOM; OINTMENT; LABORATORY; DENTISTRY; MIDWIFE

ANAGRAMS p. 136

BUILDING; CORNICE; MODERNISM; COLUMN; BASILICA; BUTTRESS; KEYS-TONE; COLONNADE; PYRAMID; SKYSCRAPER

BASKETBALL IN NEW YORK p. 137

You need at least seven ball moves to reach B from A:
- orange ball in basket #3
- green ball in basket #3
- purple ball in basket #3
- blue ball in basket #2
- yellow ball in basket #2
- purple ball in basket #1
- yellow ball in basket #1

BASKETBALL IN NEW YORK p. 138

You need at least eight ball moves to reach B from A:
- purple ball in basket #3
- orange ball in basket #3
- green ball in basket #3
- yellow ball in basket #2
- green ball in basket #1
- yellow ball in basket #1
- blue ball in basket #3
- yellow ball in basket #2

SOLUTIONS level#2

WHAT IS THE DIFFERENCE? p. 143

199

WHAT IS THE DIFFERENCE? p. 144

SOLUTIONS level#2

POINTS OF VIEW p. 145

You would be at location #1.

POINTS OF VIEW p. 146

You would be at location #3.

THE MYSTERY WORD p. 147

ARCHIVE; REPTILE; COMPANY; HIGHWAY

THE MYSTERY WORD p. 148

SEAPLANE; MOUNTAIN; CONCERTO; COLLECTOR

DECIPHER p. 153

"It's a great thing when you realize you still have the ability to surprise yourself." (*American Beauty*)

"Real loss is only possible when you love something more than you love yourself." (*Good Will Hunting*)

DECIPHER p. 154

"Every time you hear a bell ring, it means that some angel just got his wings." (*It's a Wonderful Life*)

"What's the meaning of goodness if there isn't a little badness to overcome?" (*National Velvet*)

PLAY ON WORDS p. 155

affirmative - negative
forward - backward
below - above
night - day
agnostic - religious

shy - bold
seek - avoid
remember - forget
tame - wild
infantile - mature

SOLUTIONS level#2

clueless is not a synonym of the four other words.
sunlight is not a synonym of the four other words.
divinity is not a synonym of the four other words.
sharpen is not a synonym of the four other words.

PLAY ON WORDS p. 156

prevent - permit
wise - foolish
handy - inconvenient
homozygous - heterozygous
break - repair

peace - war
harmony - dissonance
despair - hope
smooth - rough
malodorous - fragrant

wondering is not a synonym of the four other words.
common is not a synonym of the four other words.
true is not a synonym of the four other words.
deleted is not a synonym of the four other words.

WHO AM I? p. 157

I am D. H. Lawrence.

WHO AM I? p. 158

I am Kofi Annan.

SLEIGHT OF HAND p. 159

1: right; 2: right; 3: right; 4: left; 5: left; 6: left
1: left; 2: right; 3: right; 4: left; 5: left; 6: right

SLEIGHT OF HAND p. 160

1: right; 2: left; 3: right; 4: left; 5: left; 6: right
1: left; 2: left; 3: right; 4: right; 5: right; 6: left

201

SOLUTIONS level#2 ————————

NO PROBLEM! p. 161

Problem #1

5 + 5 = 10
After each hour, the discrepancy grows an additional 10 minutes.
3:30 p.m. − 12 p.m. = 3h30
Now the discrepancy is 3h30, i.e. 210 minutes.
210 ÷ 10 = 21
It has been 21 hours since the clocks were reset.
21 × 5 = 105
Therefore, the clock in the kitchen is 105 minutes fast and the living-room clock is 105 minutes slow, i.e. 1h45.
12 p.m. + 1h45 = 3:45 p.m. − 1h45 = 1:45 p.m.
It is therefore 1:45 p.m.

Problem #2

Here is the fastest solution:
Pete and Mark must leave first.
2 × 4 = 8
It will take them 8 minutes.
Then Peter, the fastest of the two, brings the boat back in four minutes.
Then Ivan and Juliana go.
8 × 2 × 2 = 32
It takes them thirty-two minutes.
The fastest of the three, Mark, brings the boat back in eight minutes.
Then Pete and Mark cross again in eight minutes.
8 + 4 + 32 + 8 + 8 = 60
So it takes the four friends sixty minutes to cross the river, which is indeed one hour. Therefore Pete was right!

NO PROBLEM! p. 162

Problem #1

If y is the volume of corn that can be put in a bag, the initial volume of corn is:
6/7 × y × 8
After the sale, there remains one-third of the corn, i.e.:

SOLUTIONS level#2 ────────────

$1/3 \times 6/7 \times y \times 8 = 16/7 \times y$ corn
and $16/7 = 2.3$
$2.3 > 2$
So two bags are not enough to store the remaining corn.

Problem #2

If wire hangers 8 and 15 cross each other that means that the wire hanger that is half their way on the cable is at one end of the cable.
It is wire hanger 12.
Also, if wire hangers 81 and 92 cross each other that means that the wire hanger that is half their way on the cable is at the other end of the cable.
It is wire hanger 87.
$87 - 12 = 75$
The two wire hangers, each at one end of the cable, are 75 wire hangers apart.
$75 \times 2 = 150$
Therefore, there are 150 wire hangers on the cable.